The HADÎQATU' L-HAQÎQAT

# THE ENCLOSED GARDEN
# OF THE TRUTH

by HAKÎM ABÛ' L-MAJD MAJDÛD SANÂÎ OF GHAZNA.

EDITED AND TRANSLATED BY

J. STEPHENSON

I0083210

THE FIRST BOOK

OF THE

*HADÎQATU' L-HAQÎQAT*

OR THE

# ENCLOSED GARDEN OF THE TRUTH

OF THE

HAKÎM ABÛ' L-MAJD MAJDÛD SANÂ'Î OF GHAZNA.

EDITED AND TRANSLATED BY

MAJOR J. STEPHENSON,
*Indian Medical Service, Member of the Royal Asiatic Society, and of the
Asiatic Society of Bengal.*

# PREFACE.

Several years ago, on looking up the literature pertaining to the earlier Sufi poets of Persia, I found that there was no European edition or translation, nor even any extended account of the contents of any of the works of Sanâ'î. Considering the reputation of this author, and the importance of his writings for the history of Sufiism, the omission was remarkable; and I was encouraged by Dr. E. D. Ross, Principal of the Calcutta. Madrasah, to do something towards filling up the blank. The present volume is an attempt at a presentation of a part of Sanâ'î's most famous work, which, it is hoped. may serve to give an idea of his manner of thought not only to Oriental scholars, but also to non-Orientalists who may be interested in the mysticism of Persia.

MSS. of Sanâ'î's Ḥadîqa are not rare in European libraries and a selection of those contained in the British Museum and India Office libraries furnished me with as many as I was able to collate during the time I could devote to this work on the occasion of a recent furlough. My selection of MSS. for collation was, I must confess, somewhat arbitrary C I took because it was the oldest of those to which I had access H because it also was of respectable age, and fairly well written; M mainly on account of its being easily legible, this being a consideration, since; my time in London was limited, and the British Museum does not allow MSS. to leave the building; I I took because it was written in Iṣfahân and so might embody a Persian, as distinct from an Indian, tradition of the text; and A was selected because it was stated to be `Abdu'l-Laṭîf's autograph of his revision of the text. I must here acknowledge my gratitude to the management of the India Office Library for the permission accorded me to take away these two valuable MSS. for collation in the country; the materials upon which the present text is based would otherwise have been much poorer, and the result even more inconclusive than it is.

Though thus in some degree arbitrary, and restricted to only two collections, I do not think a limited choice of MSS. could have turned out much more fortunately. It has at least, I think, brought a considerable amount of light to bear on the history of the author's text, especially with regard to the labours of its editor `Abdu'l-Laṭîf in the seventeenth century; though, as explained in the Introduction, I am very far from imagining that we have arrived at any close approximation to the author's original. I do not say that a reconstruction of Sanâ'î's original text is impossible; though judging merely from the MSS. I have examined, I am inclined to doubt the possibility. The text fell into confusion at a very early date, and it will perhaps only be by prolonged search or by a lucky chance that a future editor will obtain a copy which approximates in any close degree to the original; though a closer and more prolonged study of the copies we possess would, I have no doubt, give indications as to the place of many lines and passages which in the present edition are almost certainly wrongly placed or have been set apart as homeless. But at the present stage of Oriental studies it is unprofitable to devote to the preparation of a text the same prolonged research which we are accustomed to see in editions of the classical authors of Greece and Rome; and the labour of scholars in the province of Oriental letters is better expended on a first rough survey of the ground, so much of which remains as yet absolutely unknown; when a general knowledge of the whole has been obtained, it will be time to return for a thorough cultivation of each individual plot.

In the list of the variant readings I have found it quite impossible to indicate the different order of the lines and sections in the several MSS., nor have I as a rule given the variations in the titles of the sections. Otherwise the list is complete.

The translation is as literal as I have been able to make it. The notes are largely taken from the commentaries of `Abdu'l-Laṭîf, published along with the text in the Lucknow lithograph (L), and of `Alâu'd-Dîn, similarly given in the lithograph (B) which I obtained from Bombay. I have utilized all such portions of these commentaries as appeared to me to be helpful in arriving at an understanding of the text; matter taken from the commentary in the Lucknow lithograph I have distinguished by the letter L, also used in the list of variants to denote the readings of this lithograph; similarly the matter of `Alâu'd-Dîn's commentary is distinguished in the notes by the letter B. Where the note presents a literal translation of the commentaries, I have indicated this by the use of inverted commas; where my note gives only the general sense of the commentary I have omitted the quotation marks, the source of the note being sufficiently indicated by the appropriate letter.

In the fuller explanation of the technicalities of Sufi. philosophy I have drawn largely on the first volume of the late E. J. W. Gibb's "History of Ottoman Poetry," and especially on the second chapter of that work; where allusions to proper names, etc., are not explained by the commentators, I have often quoted from Hughes's "Dictionary of Islam." Quotations from the Qur'ân I have usually given in Palmer's translation. Finally, I am myself responsible for the notes in cases where no source is given; these are usually either in places where the meaning of the text is not easy to grasp, and where nevertheless the commentators, as not infrequently happens, pass over the line without explanation; or on the other hand such notes refer to matters of common knowledge to Persian scholars, which however may not be familiar to others; I have added a certain number of such in order, as stated already, to render the work of some use to non-Persianists who take an interest in the philosophies of the East.

Had I been able to devote myself continuously to the work, the number of references from one part of the text to another might have been considerably increased, and the author's meaning probably in many places thus rendered clearer; I think also, as I have already said, lines and passages that are here doubtless misplaced might have found, if not their original, still a more suitable home. But it has often happened that months, in one case as many as eleven, have elapsed between putting down the work and taking it up again; and thus all but the most general remembrance of the contents of the earlier parts of the text has in the meanwhile escaped me. I can only say that it seemed better to let the work go out as it is, than to keep it longer in the hope of obtaining a continuous period of leisure which may never come, for a more thorough revision and recasting of the whole.

GOVERNMENT COLLEGE,
LAHORE:
*June* 1908.

## ABBREVIATIONS.

L (in the notes) refers to the commentary of 'Abdu'l-Latîf.

* (in the notes) refers to the commentary of 'Alâu'd-Dîn.

Gibb = A History of Ottoman Poetry, vol. I, by E. J. W. Gibb. London. Luzac & Co., 1900.

Sale = Sale's Translation of the Qur'ân, with notes (several editions; a cheap one is published by Warne & Co.).

Stein. =Steingass's Persian-English Dictionary.

B.Q. = *The Burhân-i Qâti*` (a Persian Dictionary, in Persian).

The scheme of transliteration adopted is that at present sanctioned by the Asiatic Society of Bengal.

The references in the notes to other passages of the work are given according to the page and line of the Persian text (indicated also in the margin of the translation).

Quotations from the Arabic ore indicated by printing in italics.

# CONTENTS

# I.--LIFE OF THE AUTHOR.

Abû'l-Majd Majdûd b. Adam Sanâ'î [1] was born at Ghazna, and lived in the reign of Bahrâmshâh (A.H. 512-548, A.D. 1118-1152). Ouseley says of him that he "while yet young became one of the most learned, devout, and excellent men of the age which he adorned. His praise was on every tongue; for, in addition to his accomplishments in the Sufi philosophy, he possessed a kind and benevolent heart, delightful manners, and a fine taste for poetry . . . . Sanâî in early life retired from the world and its enjoyments, and the reason for his doing so is supposed to have arisen from the following circumstance.

"He had frequented the courts of kings and princes, and celebrated their virtue and generous actions. When Sultan Ibrahim of Ghazni determined upon attacking the infidel idolaters of India, Hakim Sanâî composed a poem in his praise, and was hurrying to the court to present it before that monarch's departure. There was at that time in Ghazni a madman known as Lâi Khûr (the ox-eater), who often in his incoherent wanderings uttered sentiments and observations worthy of a sounder head-piece; he was addicted to drinking wine, and frequented the bath. It so happened that Sanâî, in passing a garden, heard the notes of a song, and stopped to listen. After some time the singer, who was Lâi Khûr, addressing the cup-bearer, said, 'Saki, fill a bumper, that I may drink to the blindness of our Sultan, Ibrahim.' The Saki remonstrated and said it was wrong to wish that so just a king should become blind. The madman answered that he deserved blindness for his folly in leaving so fine a city as Ghazni, which required his presence and care, to go on a fool's errand in such a severe winter. Lâi Khûr then ordered the Saki to fill another cup, that he might drink to the blindness of Hakim Sanaî. The cup-bearer still more strongly remonstrated against this, urging the universally esteemed character of the poet, whom everyone loved and respected. The madman contended that Sanâî merited the malediction even more than the king, for with all his science and learning, he yet appeared ignorant of the purposes for which the Almighty had created him; and when he shortly came before his Maker, and was asked what he brought with him, he could only produce panegyrics on kings and princes,--

---

[1] For the facts contained in the following sketch I am indebted to Sir Gore Ouseley's "Biographical Notices of the Persian Poets," Lond., Or. Trans. Fund, 1846; Rieu's and Ethé's Catalogues; and Prof. Browne's "A Literary History of Persia," Vol. II.

mortals like himself. These words made so deep an impression on the sensitive mind of the pious philosopher, that he secluded himself from the world forthwith, and gave up all the luxuries and vanities of courts.

"Sirâjuddin Ali, in his 'Memoirs of the Poets,' says, that in consequence of the sudden impression occasioned by Lâi Khûr's remarks, Sanâî sought instruction from the celebrated Sheikh Yusef Hamdani, whose cell was called the 'Kaabah of Khorâsân.'

"It was about this time that Behrâm Shah offered him his sister in marriage, which honour, however, he gratefully declined, and almost immediately set out on a pilgrimage to Mecca and Medinah. It is to the refusal of the royal bride that he alludes in his Hedîkeh, as an apology to the king, in the following lines:--'I am not a person desirous of gold or of a wife, or of exalted station; by my God, I neither seek them nor wish them. If through thy grace and favour thou wouldest even offer me thy crown, I swear by thy head I should not accept it.'" The account of Sanâ'î's conversion contained in the foregoing extract is probably, as Browne says, of little historical value.

Sanâ'î composed the present work after his return from the pilgrimage; according to most copies he completed it in A.H. 525 (A.D. 1131), though some MSS. have A.H. 534 or 535 (A.D. 11391141).

Sanâ'î was attacked during his lifetime on account of his alleged unorthodoxy; but a fatwa was published by the Khalîfa's court at Baghdâd, vindicating his orthodoxy against his calumniators. His commentator `Abdu'l-Latîf, if in his Preface (v. post.) mentions the suspicions of the various sects on the subject of the Hakîm's heresies.

Several dates are given for the Hakîm's death. His disciple Muhammad b. `Ali al-Raffâ (Raqqâm), in a preface to the work preserved in one of the Bodleian MSS., gives Sunday, the 11th Sha`bân A.H. 525 (A.D. 1131). This date, however, fell on a Thursday; the 11th Sha`bân of the year A.H. 545 (A.D. 1150), which is the date given by Taqî Kâshî and the Âtashkada, was, however, a Sunday. Daulatshâdh and Hâjî Khalfa give A.H. 576 (A.D. 1180, 1181). Since the poet completed his Tarîqu't-Tahqîq in A.H. 528, the earliest of the three dates is impossible; the second would appear -to be the most probable.

Besides the Hadîqatu'l-Haqîqat, the first chapter of which is here presented, Sanâ'î wrote the Tarîqu't-Tahqîq ("Path of Verification"), Gharîb-nâma ("Book of the Stranger"), Sairu'l- `ibâd ila'l-Ma`âd ("Pilgrimage of [God's] servants to the Hereafter"), Kâr-nâma Book of Deeds "), `Ishq-nâma (" Book of Love "), and *'Aql-nâma* ("Book of Reason"), as well as a *Dîwân*, or collection of shorter poems in various metres. All these works, with the exception of the *Haqîqa* and the *Dîwân*, are said by Prof. Browne, from whom the above list is taken, to be very rare.

## II.--MANUSCRIPTS AND LITHOGRAPHS.

I have used the following manuscripts and lithographs in the preparation of the text:--

(I) Br. Mus. Add. 25329. Foll. 298, 7 ¾" x 4 ¾", 15 ll. 2 3/8" long, in small Nestalik, with gold headings, dated Safar A.H. 890 (A.D. 1485) [Adam Clarke].

There are marginal additions by two other hands; f. I is on different paper, by a different and later hand. The letters #, #, #, # are often not distinguished, # never; # and # are often not distinguished from # and #; the small letters are often without dots; the scribe usually writes the modern undotted # with three dots below. There are large omissions as compared with later MSS. and the lithographs.

I denote this MS. by C.

(2) Br. Mus. Or. 358. Foll. 317, 6 ¾" x 3 ¾", 17 ll. 2" long, in small Nestalik, in two gold-ruled columns, with two 'unvâns, apparently written in the 16th cent. [Geo. Wm. Hamilton].

There are many marginal additions, mostly by one, a later, hand,: the MS. as a whole has been subjected to a great many erasures and corrections. The writing is good, the pointing of the letters fairly complete; the scribe usually writes and the # and #, the # rarely appears with three dots below. The MS. contains the prefaces of Raqqâm and of Sanâ'î himself, but, like the preceding, shows omissions as compared with later MSS. and the lithographs.

I denote this MS. by H.

(3) Br. Mus. Add. 16777. Foll. 386, 10 ¾" x 6 ¼", 15 ll., 3 ½" long, in fair Nestalik, with gold-ruled margins, dated A.H. 1076 (A.D. 1665) [Win. Yule].

This is a clearly written MS., the pointing of the letters usually full, #, and, # are frequently distinguished by their dots, and the pure # usually written with three dots below. Erasures are not frequent; the marginal corrections usually by the original hand. This MS. gives a very large number of divergent readings as compared with the others; its order is very different from that of the others; it is, as regards its extent, not so much defective as redundant, long passages appearing twice, and some passages not to be found in any of my other sources are also included. Some of these latter I have found in subsequent chapters of the Ḥadîqa, and it is possible that a more thorough search might have shown that they are all contained there.

This MS. is denoted by M.

(4) Ind. Off. 918. Ff. 395, 2 coll. each ll. 15; Nastaʿlîk; the last four pp. written by another hand; 9 ½" by 5 ½". Written at Iṣfahân A.H. 1027 (A.D. 1618); occasional short glosses on the margin.

A clearly written and well-preserved MS., closely related to the following. The letters # and #, are frequently distinguished; the sign *madda*, is usually omitted.

I denote this MS. by I.

(5) Ind. Off. 923. The description given in the Catalogue is as follows -- "Sharḥ-Ḥadîkah. The revised and collated edition of Sanâʾî's Ḥadîkah with a commentary and marginal glosses by ʿAbd-allaṭîf bin ʿAbdallâh al-ʿAbbâsî, who is best known by his revised and annotated edition of Jalâl-aldîn Rûmi's Mathnawî, his commentaries on the same poem, and a special glossary, Laṭâʾf-allughât (lithogr. Lucknow under title Farhang-i-Mathnawî 1877). He died 1048 or 1049 (A.D. 1638, 1639) in Shahjahân's reign. The present copy, which is the author's autograph, was finished by him 20th Jumâdâ alawwal A.H. 1044 (=Nov. 11th, 1634), and represents an abridgement from a larger commentary of his, the Laṭâʾif al Ḥadâʾiḳ, from which also the glosses are taken (marked #). According to the dîbâca he began the larger work 1040 and completed it 1042 (1630-33) supported by his friend Mîr ʿImâd-aldîn Maḥmûd al Hamadânî, with the takhalluṣ Ilâhî, the author of the well-known tadhkirah of Persian poets the Khazîna-i-Ganj.'

The following is an account of the contents of this MS. First comes a short preface by ʿAbduʾl-Laṭîf, introducing Sanâʾî's own preface, which is stated to have been written to the complete collection of his writings; it is frequently, states ʿAbduʾl-Laṭîf, not to be found in copies of his works. After Sanâʾî's preface comes another, called *Râsta-i khiyâbân*, by ʿAbduʾl-Laṭîf, described as a short preface to this writer's commentary; this concludes with a reference to

Ilâhî and his share in the work, and two *târîkhs* by Ilâhî, giving A.H. 1040 as the date of its commencement, and 1042 as that of its completion. A few more lines by `Abdu'l-Latîf introduce the work itself. The original numbering of the folia commences with the text; there is also a pencil numbering, in English characters, beginning with the first preface The poem closes with 59 verses, in the same metre, which form an address to Abû'l-Hasan `Alî b. Nâsir al Ghaznawî, named Biryângar, sent to him at Baghdâd, because of the accusations of the traducers of the book. The date of completion of the text is given as A.H. 535; and, in a triangular enclosure of gold lines, it is stated that "this honoured copy was completed 20th Jumâdâ al-awwal, 1044 A.H." A few pages at the end, written by the same hand, give an account of how the book was sent to Biryângar at Baghdâd, on account of the accusations that were brought against it; how it was found to be orthodox, and a reply sent to Ghaznî.

This MS. I denote by A.

(6) The Lucknow lithograph published by the Newal Kishore Press, dated A.H. 1304 (A.D. 1886). This is an edition of the whole, work, including prefaces and `Abdu'l-Latîf's commentary. It comprises 860 pp., of 15 verses to a page; the paper, as usual, is somewhat inferior; the text is on the whole easily legible, but the same cannot always be said for the commentary, written in the margins and in a much smaller hand. It contains first a list of the titles of all the sections of all the chapters, followed by some verses setting forth the subjects of the ten chapters each as a whole. The ornamental title-page follows, stating that the *Hadîqa* of Sanâ'î is here accompanied by the commentary *Latâ'ifu'l-Hadâ'iq* of `Abdu'l-Latîf al-`Abbâsî. On p. 2 begins the 'First Preface', called *Mirâtu'l-Hadâ'iq*, by 'Abdu'l-Latîf, dated 1038 A. H.; this is not included in A; an abstract of it is given later (v. p. xxi). After this comes Sanâ'î's preface with `Abdu'l-Latîf's introductory words, as in A; this is called the 'Second Preface'. The 'Third Preface', which is `Abdu'l-Latîf's *Râsta-i khiyâbân*, is here written in the margins of the ' Second Preface'. Then comes the text with marginal commentary, introduced as in A by a few more words from `Abdu'l-Latîf. At the conclusion of the work is the address to Biryângar; and finally some *qit`as* on the dates of commencement and completion of the printing of the book.

I denote this lithograph by L.

(7) I obtained from Bombay, from the bookshop of Mirzâ Muhammad Shîrâzî, another lithograph, which comprises only the first chapter of the work accompanied by a copious marginal commentary. Pp. 15 + 4 + 31 + 188, 15 ll. to a page; published at Lûhârû (near Hissar, Punjab) 1290 A.H. (1873

17

A.D.). The title-page states that this is the commentary on Sanâ'î's Ḥadîqa by Nawâb Mirzâ `Alâu'd-Dîn Aḥmad, Khân Bahâdur, chief (###) of Lûhârû, called `Alâ'î, the scribe being Maulavî Muḥammad Ruknu'd-Dîn of Ḥiṣṣar. Ruknu'd-Dîn states (p. 2) that he himself was doubtful of many words, and did not understand a number of the verses; he took his difficulties to `Alâ'î, who explained all; and "Praise be to God, there never has been such a commentator of the Ḥadîqa, nor will be; or if there is, it will be an imitation or a theft from this king of commentators." This reads rather curiously when considered in connection with the fact, to be mentioned hereafter, that the authors have incorporated in their commentary the whole of that of `Abdu'l-Laṭîf, and that their original contributions to the elucidation of the text are of slight value. Ruknu'd-Dîn was asked one day by the printers (###) to bring them his copy (###) of the Ḥadîqa on its completion, for printing and publication. Pp. 4-10 are occupied by an Arabic preface by Ruknu'd-Dîn, again in extravagant praise of `Alâ'î and his accomplishments as a commentator. There follows (pp. 11-14) another title-page, and a short poem by `Alâ'î; and then (p. 15) a qiṭ`a, giving the dates of commencement and completion of the work. Four pages of introduction (pp. 1-4) follow, and again with separate paging, 31 pp. of commentary on the first 28 pp. of the text, the reason apparently being that the whole of the commentary on these pages could not conveniently be written in the margins. The text comprises 186 pp., and includes (though I cannot find this stated anywhere) only the first book of the complete Ḥadîqa; the volume is concluded by some lines of `Alâ'î in praise of Muḥammad, and a benediction. At the end of the marginal notes on every page is written " `Alâ'î sallamahu," or "Maulânâ `Alâ'î sallamahu Allâhu ta `âla."

# III.--HISTORY OF THE TEXT.

Muḥammad b. ʿAlî Raqqâm informs us, in his preface to the *Hadîqa*, that while Sanâ'î was yet engaged in its composition, some portions were abstracted and divulged by certain ill-disposed persons. Further, ʿAbdu'l-Laṭîf in his preface, the *Mirâtu'l-Ḥadâ'iq*, states that the disciples of Sanâ'î made many different arrangements of the text, each one arranging the matter for himself and making his own copy; and that thus there came into existence many and various arrangements, and two copies agreeing together could not be found.

The confusion into which the text thus fell is illustrated to some extent by the MSS. which I have examined for the purpose of this edition. C shows many omissions as compared with later MSS.; at the same time there is a lengthy passage, 38 verses, which is not found in any other; H, though also defective, is fuller than C but evidently belongs to the same family. M contains almost all the matter comprised in ʿAbdu'l-Laṭîf's recension, much of it twice over as has already been mentioned; and in addition about 300 verses, or altogether 10 folia, which apparently do not of right belong to this first chapter at all; the first chapter, too, is here divided into two chapters. The remaining MSS. and lithographs agree closely with each other and are evidently all nearly related.

The same story, of an early confusion of the text, is even more strikingly brought out if, instead of the omissions and varying extent of the text in the several MSS., we compare the order of the text. Here M startles us by giving us an order totally at variance with that of any other of our sources. There seems to be no reason for this: the arrangement of the subject is not, certainly, more logical; and it would appear that the confusion has simply been due to carelessness at some early stage of the history of the text; the repetitions, and the inclusions of later parts of the work, point to the same explanation. I need only mention the consequent labour and expenditure of time on the collation of this manuscript. C and H agree mostly between themselves in the order of the text, and broadly speaking the general order is the same as that of the later MSS.; the divergences would no doubt have appeared considerable, but that they are entirely overshadowed by the confusion exhibited by M. IALB agree closely with each other, as before.

The same confusion is again seen in the titles of the various sections as given in the several MSS. I am inclined to doubt how far any of the titles are to be considered as original; and it seems to me very possible that all are later additions, and that the original poem was written as one continuous whole, not divided up into short sections as we have it now. At any rate, the titles vary very much in the different MSS.; some, I should say, were obviously marginal glosses transferred to serve as headings; in other cases the title has reference only to the first few lines of the section, and is quite inapplicable to the subject-matter of the bulk of the section; in other cases again it is difficult to see any applicability whatever. It appears to have been the habit of the copyists to leave spaces for the titles, which were filled in later; in some cases this has never been done .. in others, through some omission in the series, each one of a number of sections will be denoted by a title which corresponds to that of the text following section in other MSS.

It is then obvious that `Abdu'l-Latîf is right in saying that in the centuries following Sanâ'î's death great confusion existed in the text of the *Hadîqa*. This text he claims to have purified and restored, as well as explained by means of his commentary; and it is his recension which is given in A, as well as in the Indian lithographs L and B. He says that he heard that the Nawâb Mirzâ Muhammad `Azîz Kaukiltâsh, styled the Great Khân, had, while governor of Gujrât in the year 1000 A.H., sent to the town of Ghaznîn a large sum of money in order to obtain from the tomb of Sanâ'î a correct copy of the *Hadîqa*, written in an ancient hand; this copy the Nawâb, on his departure on the pilgrimage, had bestowed on the Amîr `Abdu'r-Razzâq Ma`mûri, styled Muzaffar Khan, at that time viceroy of that country. `Abdu'l-Latîf, however, being then occupied in journeys in various parts of India, could not for some time present himself before the Amîr; till in A.H. 1035 this chief came to Agra, where `Abdu'l-Latîf presented himself before him and obtained the desire of so many years. This MS. of the *Hadîqa* had been written only 80 years after the original composition, but the text did not satisfy the editor, and it was besides deficient, both in verses here and there, and also as regards twenty leaves in the middle of the work.

In the year A.H. 1037 `Abdu'l-Latîf came to Lahore, where having some freedom from the counterfeit affairs of the world and the deceitful cares of this life, he entered again on the task of editing the text, with the help of numerous copies supplied to him by learned and critical friends; He adopted the order of the ancient MS. before-mentioned, and added thereto such other verses as he found in the later MSS. which appeared to be of common origin, and to harmonize in style and dignity and doctrine, with the text. As to what `Abdu'l-Latîf attempted in his commentary, v. p. xxii *post.*

So far `Abdu'l-Latîf's own account of his work. We can, however, supplement this by a number of conclusions derived from the MSS. themselves.

In the first place, it appears that A is not, as stated in the India Office Catalogue, `Abdu'l-Latîf's autograph copy. The statement that it is so is apparently based on the fact of the occurrence of the words "_harrarahu wa sawwadahu_ `Abdu'l-La_t_îf. b. 'Abdu'llâhi'l-`Abbâsî," at the end of the editor's few words of introduction to Sanâ'î's preface and again of the occurrence of the words "_harrarahu_ `Abdu'l-La_t_îf . . . ki _shârih_ wa niusa_hhih_-i în kitâb-i maimunat ni_s_âb ast," at the end of the few lines of introduction immediately preceding the text. But both these sentences are found in the Lucknow lithograph, and therefore must have been copied in all the intermediate MSS. from `Abdu'l-La_t_îf's autograph downwards the words in each case refer only to the paragraph to which they are appended, and were added solely to distinguish these from Sanâ'î's own writings.

I cannot find any other facts in favour of the statement that A is the editor's autograph; there are, however, many against it. Thus A is beautifully written, and is evidently the work of a skilled professional scribe, not of a man of affairs and a traveller, which `Abdu'l-La_t_îf represents himself as having been. Again, there are occasional explanatory glosses to the commentary, in the original hand; these would have been unnecessary had the scribe been himself the author of the commentary. The handwriting is quite modern in character and the pointing is according to modern standards throughout; the late date of A is immediately brought out clearly by comparing it with I (of date 1027 A.H.) or M (of date 1076 A.H.); though the supposed date of A is 1044 A.H. it is obviously much later than either of the others. But perhaps the most curious bit of evidence is the following; at the top of fol. 11*b* of the text of A there is an erasure, in which is written #### in place of an original reading ####, and as it happens this line is one which has been commented on by the editor; in the margin is a note in a recent hand,--####, which is true,--the commentary certainly presumes a reading ####, but this MS. had originally ####; the scribe could not therefore have been the commentator himself, i.e., `Abdu'l-La_t_îf

Further, not only is A not `Abdu'l-La_t_îf's autograph, but it does not accurately reproduce that autograph. I refer to 34 short passages of Sanâ'î's text, which in A are found as additions in the margin; these, though obviously written in the same hand, I regard as subsequent additions from another source by the same scribe, not as careless omissions filled in afterwards on comparing the copy with the original. In the first place, the scribe was on the whole a careful writer; and the mistakes he has made in transcribing the commentary, apart from the text, are few. The omissions of words or passages of commentary, which have been filled in afterwards, are altogether 10; of these, two are of single words only; two are on the first page, when perhaps the copyist had not thoroughly settled down to his work; five are short passages, no doubt due to carelessness; and one is a longer passage, the whole of a comment on a certain verse,--an example of carelessness certainly, but explicable by supposing that the scribe had overlooked the reference number in the text indicating that the comment was to be introduced in relation to that particular verse. Roughly speaking, the commentary is of about equal bulk with the text; yet the omissions of portions of commentary by the copyist are thus many fewer in number and much less in their united extent than the omissions of the text,--supposing, that is, that the marginal additions to the text in A are merely the consequence of careless copying. The reverse would be expected, since owing to the manner of writing, it is easier to catch up the place where one has got to in a verse composition; it would seem therefore. as said above, that the comparatively numerous marginal additions to the text are rather additions introduced afterwards from another source than merely careless omissions in copying. In the second place, none of these 34 passages are annotated by `Abdu'l-Laṭîf; in all likelihood, if they had formed part of his text, some one or more of the lines would have received a comment. The passages comprise, together, 63 verses; there is only one instance in the First chapter of the _Hadîqa_ of a longer consecutive passage without annotation, and in general it is rare (eleven instances only) to find more than 30 consecutive verses without annotation; usually the editor's comments occur to the number of two, three or more on each page of 15 lines. I think, therefore. it must be admitted that the chances would be much against a number of casual omissions aggregating 63 lines falling out so as not to include a single comment of the editor. Thirdly, it is a remarkable fact that of these 34 passages the great majority are also omitted in both C and H, while they are present in both M and I; to particularize, C omits 30 ½, H omits 28, both C and H omit 25 ½, and either C or H or both omit every one of these 34 passages; while I and M each have all the 34 with one exception in each case; further, while many of these 34 marginally added passages in A correspond exactly to omissions in H, the corresponding omissions in C may be more extensive, i.e., may include more, in each case, of the neighbouring text.

We must therefore, I think, conclude that after completing the transcription of A the scribe obtained a copy of the _Hadîqa_ of the type of I or M, and filled in certain additions therefrom; and that '`Abdu'l-Laṭîf's edition did not originally contain these passages.

Let us turn to a consideration of I and its relation to `Abdu'l-Laṭîf's edition. I is dated A.H. 1027; it is, therefore, earlier than `Abdu'l-Laṭîf's edition of A.H. 1044. As we have seen, A is not `Abdu'l-Laṭîf's autograph; but we have, I think, no reason to doubt that it was either copied from that autograph, or at any rate stands in the direct line of descent; so much seems to be attested by the occurrence of the words --"_ḥarrarahu `Abdu'l-Laṭîf_ . . . . . . " and by the inscription at the end as to the completion of the book in A.H. 1044, the actual date of the completion of `Abdu'l-Laṭîf's work. Regarding, then, A as presenting us (with the exception of the marginally added passages) with a practically faithful copy of `Abdu'l-Laṭîf's own text, we notice a striking correspondence between this text and that of I. As to the general agreement of the readings of the two texts, a glance at the list of variants will be sufficient; and it is not impossible to find whole pages without a single difference of any importance. The titles also, which as a rule vary even so much in the different MSS., correspond closely throughout. The order of the sections is the same throughout; and the order of the lines within each section, which, ' is also very variable in the various M88., corresponds in I and A with startling closeness. The actual spellings of individual words also, which vary even in the same MS., are frequently the same in I and A; for example, at the bottom of p. #### of the present text the word #### or #### occurs three times within a few lines. The word may also be written ####, ####; thus while C and M have ####, H has first #### and then twice ####; I however has first #### and then twice ####; and this is exactly repeated in A. Another example occurs a few lines afterwards (p. ####, l. ####); the reading is ####, *mâr-i shikanj*, *mâr* being followed by the izâdfat; this I writes as ####; in A an erasure occurs between #### and ####, doubtless due to the removal of a #### originally written there as in I.

The above will serve to show the close relation between I and A, or between I and `Abdu'l-Laṭîf's autograph, of which A is a copy or descendant. But, however close this relationship, `Abdu'l-Laṭîf cannot actually have used I in the preparation of his revision of the text, or he would certainly have incorporated many of the 34 passages before alluded to, which were all, with one exception, contained in I. These, we have seen, were only added by the scribe of A, and by him only subsequently, from another source, after he had completed his transcription from `Abdu'l-Laṭîf's autograph.

The facts, then, are these. There was in existence, before `Abdu'l-Laṭîf's time, a tradition, probably Persian, of the order of the text, which he adopted even in detail. This is represented for us by I, written A.H. 1027 at Iṣfahân; but I itself is somewhat fuller than the copy of which `Abdu'l-Laṭîf if made such great use. This copy may be called P. Such use, indeed, did `Abdu'l-Laṭîf make of P, that, so far as can be seen, it is only necessary that he should have had P before him, with one or two other copies from which he derived a certain number of variant readings, which he substituted here and there in his own edition for those of P.

We have now brought down the history of the text to A.H. 1044. Not much remains to be said; A, as we have seen, is quite possibly a direct copy of `Abdu'l-Laṭîf's autograph, with, however, marginal additions from another source. This other source might be at once assumed to be I, but for the fact that only 33 out of the 34 marginally added passages occur in I; and it still

23

seems to me at least possible that I was thus used. I, though written at Iṣfahân, was probably by this time in India, where A, the so-called "Tippu MS.," was certainly written; at least, that I did come to India may be assumed from its presence in the India Office Library. Again, though it is, I think, impossible that the whole of the 34 passages added marginally in A should have been careless omissions of the copyist, one or two might possibly be so, and it is possible that the single line now under discussion may be such an omission, filled in from the scribe's original, not from another source. Finally it is, of course, always possible that the additions were taken from two sources, not one only; i.e., that while perhaps even 33 were filled in after comparison with I, the single remaining line may have been derived from elsewhere. Though absent in C, it is present in both H and M.

As to the lithographs, both are obviously descendants of A. The above conclusions may be summarized in the following *stemma codicum*.

24

Sanā'ī's original (534 ?).

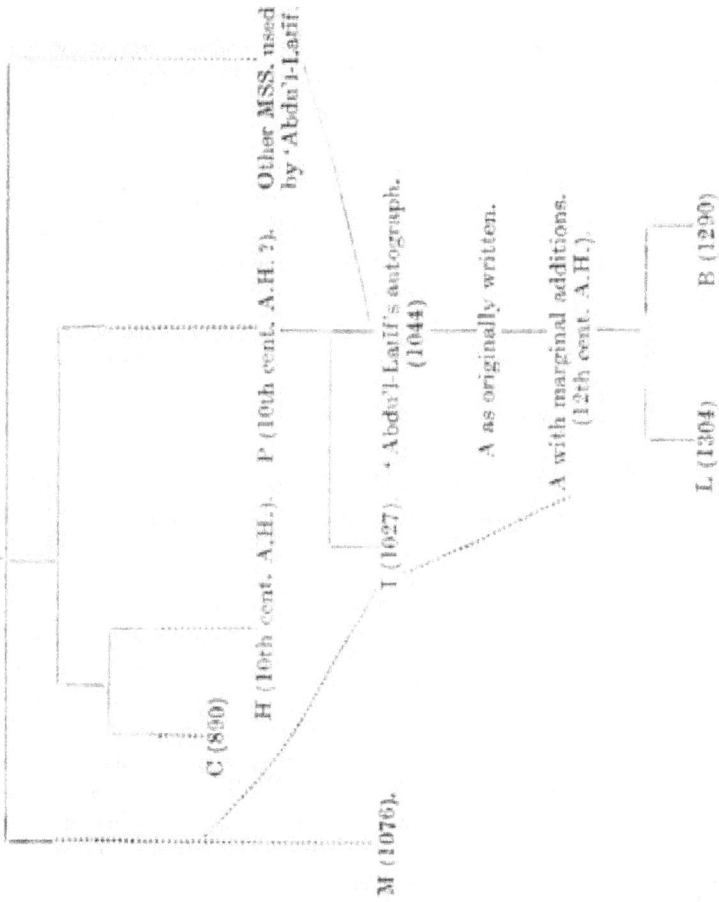

H (10th cent. A.H.).  P (10th cent. A.H. ?).  Other MSS. used by 'Abdu'l-Laṭīf.

C (890).

M (1076).

T (1027)  'Abdu'l-Laṭīf's autograph. (1044)

A as originally written.

A with marginal additions. (12th cent. A.H.).

L (1304)  B (1290)

The present text is founded on that of the Lucknow lithograph L, with which have been collated the other texts mentioned above. L is practically a verbatim copy of A, the value of which has been discussed above. Though MSS. of the _Hadíqa_ are not rare, at least in European libraries, I have not met with any in India; and a considerable portion of the first draft of the translation and notes was done on the basis of L and B alone. The _Hadíqa_ is not in any case an easy book, with the exception, perhaps, of a number of the anecdotes which are scattered through it; and it was rendered far more difficult by the fact, which I did not recognize for some time, that a very great amount of confusion exists even in the text as it is published to-day, in the lithographs descended from `Abdu'l-Latîf's recension. There appeared to be frequently no logical connection whatever between successive verses; whole pages appeared to consist of detached sayings, the very meaning of which was frequently obscure; a subject would be taken up only to be dropped immediately.

I ultimately became convinced that the whole work had fallen into confusion, and that the only way of producing any result of value would be to rearrange it. This I had done, tentatively, for part of the work, before collating the British Museum and India office MSS. cited above.

When I came to examine the MSS., the wide variations, not only in the general order of the sections to which allusion has already been made, but in the order of the verses within each section, showed me that probably no MS. at the present day, or at any rate none of those examined by me, retains the original order of the author: and I felt justified in proceeding as I had begun, altering the order of the lines, and even of the sections, if by so doing a. meaning or a logical connection could be brought out. I need not say that the present edition has no claims to represent Sanâ'î's original; probably it does not represent it even approximately. In some cases there is, I think, no doubt that I have been able to restore the original order of the lines, and so to make sense where before it was wanting; in other cases this is possible, but I feel less confident; while in still others the reconstruction, preferable though I believe it to be to the order as found in any single MS., is nevertheless almost certainly a, makeshift, and far from the original order. Lastly it will be seen that I have quite failed, in a number of instances, to find the context of short passages or single lines; it seemed impossible to allow them to stand in the places they occupied in any of the MSS., and I have, therefore, simply collected them together, or in the ease of single lines given them in the notes.

## IV.--THE COMMENTATORS.

Khwâja `Abdu'l-Latîf b. `Abdullâh al-`Abbâsî, already so frequently mentioned, explains to us in his Preface, the Mirâtu'l-Hadâ'iq, what he has attempted in his commentary on the Hadîqa. He states that he was writing in A.H. 1038, in the second year of the reign of the Emperor Shahjahân, that he had already completed his work on Jalâlu'd-Dîn Rûmî's Mathnawî, and that he had in A.H. 1037 settled down to work on the Hadîqa. 'What he professes to have done for the text of that work has been mentioned in the last section; the objects he has aimed at in the way of commentary and explanation are the following:--

Firstly, he has followed up the references to passages in the Qur'ân, has given these passages with their translations, and a statement of the sûra in which they are to be found. Secondly, the traditions referred to are also quoted. Thirdly, obscure passages have been annotated, and strange or curious Arabic and Persian words have been explained, after an investigation into their meanings in trustworthy books. Fourthly, certain signs have been used in transcribing the text, in order to fix the signification of various letters; thus the yâ'i kitâbî is denoted by ### subscript, the yâ'i majhûl similarly by ###, the yâ'i ma'rûf by ###, the Persian # (#) by #, the Arabic # by #, and so on. Again the vocalization has been attended to in words which are often mispronounced; thus ignorant people often substitute fatha for kasra in such words as 'khizâna', of which the Qâmûs says "Khizâna is never pronounced with fatha"; 'Shamâl', meaning the North wind, should be pronounced with fatha, not kasra, as is often done. The izâfat, jazm, and other orthographical signs have often been written in the text; and finally a glossary of the less known words has been added in the margin. Since it is inconvenient to have text and commentary separate, "in this copy the whole stability of the text has been dissolved, and the text bears the commentary along with it (###), i.e., text and commentary are intermingled, the commentary not being written in the margin, but each annotation immediately after the word or line to which it applies. These researches the author has also written out separately, and called them "Latâ'ifu'l-Hadâ'iq min Nafâ'isi'l-Daqâ'iq." The date is again given as A.H. 1038.

It appears then that the original form of the commentary was not that of marginal notes, as it is presented in A and L; that it was completed in 1038 A.H., and, in its separate form, was called the Latâ'ifu'l-Hadâ'iq. That this is the name of the commentary we know and possess, seems to have been the opinion of the scholar who prepared the Lucknow lithograph, which is entitled "Sanâ'î's Hadîqa, with the commentary Latâ'ifu'l-Hadâ'iq."

Besides the preface just considered, there is also another, found in both A and L, called the *Râsta-i Khiyâbân*, written especially, it would seem, as an introduction to the commentary *Latâ'ifu'l-Hadâ'iq*. After dwelling on the unworthiness of the writer, `Abdu'l-Latîf states that the interpretations given by him are not mere expressions of private opinion, but are derived from the best Arabic and Persian books; the emendations of the text are all derived from authentic MSS., and are in accordance with the judgment of discerning men; everything has been weighed and discussed by the learned. He does not, however, say that these explanations are the only ones, nor that he has commented on every line that to some people would seem to require it. Though his work may seem poor now while he is alive, it may grow in the esteem of men after his death. The work has been done in the intervals of worldly business, while occupied with affairs of government. There follows a lengthy eulogy of his friend Mîr `Imâdu'd-Dîn Mahmûd al-Hamadâni, called Ilâhî, two *târîkhs* by whom close this preface. The first *târîkh* says that the work having been begun in the year 1040. all the correction and revision was completed in 1042 (###); the second simply gives the date 1040.

These dates evidently cannot refer to the edition and commentary as first written; since we have seen that the text and the *Latâ'ifu'l-Hadâ'iq* are referred to by `Abdu'l-Latîf in 1038 as having been completed. It would seem that the editor had either been at work on another, revised and improved edition; or, as is assumed in the India Office Catalogue (No. 923), on an abridgment of his earlier work. Lastly, we have the date 1041 for the completed work of which A is a copy (see description of contents of A, in Section II, p. xi); and this seems to represent the final form of the work. in which the annotations are written in the margin, not, as at first, intermingled in the text.

In the India Office Catalogue the series of events is interpreted somewhat differently. The commentary as it appears in A (and L, the only form, apparently, in which we possess it) is stated to be an abridgement from a larger commentary, the *Latâ'ifu'l-Hadâ'iq*; according to the preface (the Catalogue states) the larger work wa-. begun in 1040 and completed in 1042. It is with diffidence that I venture to question this presentation of the facts; but A, in the description of which the above statements occur, does not contain the preface called *Mirâtu'l-Hadâ'iq*, and therefore presents no indication that the text and *Latâ'ifu'l-Hadâ'iq* had already been completed in 1038. That the work done between 1040 and 1042 consisted in the preparation of the original *Latâ'ifu'l-Hadâ'iq* is, from the statement of the *Mirâtu'l-Hadâ'iq*, impossible. We have seen, moreover, that the tradition in India is that the commentary as we have it, as it appears in A and L, is the *Latâ'ifu'l-Hadâ'iq* itself., and not an abridgement. I do not gather from the India Office Catalogue or elsewhere that two-commentaries, a larger and a smaller, are actually in existence; there may be other evidences of their former existence of which I am ignorant, but so far merely as my own knowledge goes, I can see no reason for assuming two commentaries, and would look on the labours of 1040-1042 in the light of revision and rearrangement, a work which was perhaps only finally completed in 1044, the date given in A for the completion of the work. Besides his work on the *Hadîqa*, `Abdu'l-Laṭîf had previously, as has been mentioned, published a revised and annotated edition of Jalâlu'd-Dîn Rûmî's Mathnawî, commentaries on the same poem, and a special glossary, the lithographed at Lucknow in A.D. 1877 under the title *Farhang-i Maṯẖnawî*. He died in 1048 or 1049 A.H. (A.D. 1638, 1639).

A general description of the volume containing the other commentary which I have used in the preparation of the notes appended to the present translation, has already been given. Of the authors, or author and scribe, Mirzâ `Alâu'd-Dîn Aḥmad of Lûhârû, called `Alâ'î, and Maulavî Muhammad Ruknu'd-Dîn of Hiṣṣar, I know no more, than is to be gathered from their prefaces.

Their commentary is of slight value as compared with that of `Abdu'l-Laṭîf: that is to say, that part of it which is original. The commentary is considerably more bulky than `Abdu'l-Laṭîf's, perhaps between two and three times as extensive; but it includes, without one word of acknowledgment, the whole of `Abdu'l-Laṭîf's work. This is, in the great majority of cases, reproduced verbatim; in some instances a paraphrase of `Abdu'l-Laṭîf's commentary has been attempted, and in certain of these it is plain that the authors did not understand the sense of what they paraphrased. Of their own work, a certain amount is superfluous, the sense of the text being immediately obvious; a certain amount is mere paraphrase of Sanâ'î's words: and another portion consists in an attempt to read mystical meanings into the original in passages which, as it seems, were never intended by the author to bear them. Notwithstanding these facts, I have, as will be seen, quoted freely in my notes from their commentary; for a certain portion of their work is helpful, and moreover, it seemed to me to be of interest to give in this way a specimen of present-day Indian thought and criticism in the field of Ṣûfîistic philosophy. I cannot, however, leave the subject of Sanâ'î's commentators without expressing my sorrow that scholars should have existed who were not only capable of such wholesale theft, but even lauded themselves on the results of it; witness the extravagant praise of `Alâ'î in Ruknu'd-Dîn's preface; and again the words

Praise be to God! There has never been. such a commentator of the *Hadîqa*, nor will be; or if there is. it will be an imitation or a theft from this king of commentators!" There is also no indication that the volume comprises only one out of ten chapters of the *Hadîqa*; it is everywhere implied that the. complete *Hadîqa* is presented.

## V.--THE ḤADÎQATU'L-ḤAQÎQAT.

The *Hadîqatu'l-Haqîqat*, or the "Enclosed Garden of the Truth", commonly called the *Hadîqa*, is a poem of about 11,500 lines; each line consists of two hemistichs, each of ten or eleven syllables; the bulk, therefore, is equal to about 23,000 lines of English ten-syllabled verse. It is composed in the metre #### which may be represented thus:

$$- \cup - - \mid \cup - \cup - \mid \overset{\cup\cup}{-} - \quad - \cup - - \mid \cup - \cup - \mid \overset{\cup\cup}{-} -$$

The two hemistichs of each verse rhyme; and the effect may therefore roughly be compared to that of English rhymed couplets with the accent falling on the first (instead of the second) syllable of the line, and, occasionally, an additional short syllable introduced in the last foot.

The chapter,; of which the *Hadîqa* consists treat, according to a few lines of verse at the end of the table of contents in the Lucknow edition, of the following subjects; the First, on the Praise of God, and especially on His Unity; the Second, in praise of Muḥammad; the Third, on the Understanding; the Fourth, on Knowledge; the Fifth, on Love, the Lover, and the Beloved; the Sixth, on Heedlessness; the Seventh, on Friends and Enemies, the Eighth, on the Revolution of the Heavens; the Ninth, in praise of the Emperor Shâhjahân; the Tenth, on the characters or qualities of the whole work. This, however, is not the actual arrangement of the work as presented in the volume itself; the first five chapters are as already given, but the Sixth concerns the Universal Soul; the Seventh is on Heedlessness; the Eighth on the Stars; the Ninth on Friends and Enemies; the Tenth on many matters, including the praise of the Emperor. Prof. Browne (Lit. Hist. Persia, vol. ii., p. 318) gives still another order, apparently that of an edition lithographed at Bombay in A.H. 1275 (A.D. 1859).

Sanâ'î's fame has always rested on his *Hadîqa*; it is the best known and in the East by far the most esteemed of his works; it is in virtue of this work that he forms one of the great trio of Ṣûfî teachers,--Sanâ'î, `Aṭṭâr, Jalâlu'd-Dîn Rûmî. It will be of interest to compare some of the estimates that have been formed of him and of the present work in particular.

In time he was the first of the three, and perhaps the most cordial acknowledgment of his merits conies from his successor Jalâlu'd-Dîn Rûmî. He says:--

I     left     off     boiling     while     still     half     cooked;
Hear the full account from the Sage of Ghazna."

And again--

"`Aṭṭâr     was     the     Spirit,     Sanâ'î     the     two     eyes:
We walk in the wake of Sanâ'î and `Aṭṭâr."

`Abdu'l-Laṭîf, in his preface called the *Mirâtu'l-Hadâ'iq*, enters into a somewhat lengthy comparison between Sanâ'î and Rûmî, in which he is hard put to it to avoid giving any preference to one or other. It is interesting to observe how he endeavours to keep the scales even. He begins by adverting to the greater length of the *Mathnawî* as compared with the *Hadîqa*, and compares the *Hadîqa* to an abridgement, the *Mathnawî* to a fully detailed account. Sanâ'î's work is the more compressed; he expresses in two or three verses what the *Mathnawî* expresses in twenty or thirty, `Abdu'l-Laṭîf therefore, as it would seem reluctantly, and merely on the ground of his greater prolixity, gives the palm for eloquence to Jalâlu'd-Dîn.

There is the most perfect accord between Sanâ'î and Rûmî; tile substance of their works, indeed, is in part identical. Shall it therefore be said that Rûmî stole from Sanâ'î? He asks pardon from God for expressing the thought; with regard to beggars in the spiritual world, who own a stock-in-trade of trifles, bankrupts of the road of virtue and accomplishments, this might be suspected; but to accuse the treasurers of the stores of wisdom and knowledge, the able natures of the kingdom of truth and allegory, of. plagiarism and borrowing is the height of folly and unwisdom.

With regard to style, some suppose that the verse of the *Hadîqa* is more elevated and dignified than the elegantly ordered language of the *Mathnawî*. The *Hadîqa* does indeed contain poetry of which one verse is a knapsack of a hundred *dîwâns*; nor, on account of its great height, can the hand of any intelligent being's ability reach the pinnacles of its rampart; and the saying--

"I     have     spoken     a     saying     which     is     a     whole     work;
I have uttered a sentence which is a (complete) dîwân,"

is true of the *Hadîqa*. But if the sense and style of the Maulavî be considered, there is no room for discrimination and distinction; and, since "*Thou shalt not make a distinction between any of His prophets,*" to distinguish between the positions of these two masters, who may unquestionably be called prophets of religion, has infidelity and error as its fruit. Who possesses the power of

31

dividing and discriminating between milk and sugar intermingled in one vessel? `Abdu'l-Laṭîf sums up thus "in fine, thus much one may say, that in sobriety the Hakîm is pre-eminent, and in intoxication our lord the Maulavî is superior; and that sobriety is in truth the essence of intoxication, and this intoxication the essence of sobriety."

Prof. Browne, however, places the *Hadîqa* on a far lower level than the Eastern authors quoted above. He says[2]:--"The poem is written in a halting and unattractive metre, and is in my opinion one of the dullest books in Persian, seldom rising to the level of Martin Tupper's *Proverbial Philosophy*, filled with fatuous truisms and pointless anecdotes, and as far inferior to the *Mathnawî* of Jalâlu'd-Dîn Rûmî as is Robert Montgomery's *Satan* to Milton's *Paradise Lost*."

It is of course true that to us, at least, the interest of the *Hadîqa* is largely historical, as being one of the early Persian text-books of the Ṣûfî philosophy, and as having so largely influenced subsequent writers, especially, as we have seen, the Maulavî Jalâlu'd-Dîn Rûmî. Yet I cannot butt think that Prof. Browne's opinion, which is doubtless shared by other scholars, as well as the neglect to which the *Hadîqa* has been exposed in the West, is due not to the demerits of the original text so much as to the repellent and confused state into which the text has fallen; and I would venture to hope that the present attempt at a restoration of the form and meaning of a portion of the work, imperfect in the highest degree as I cannot but acknowledge it to be, may still be of some slight service to its author's reputation among European Orientalists.

The first Chapter or Book of the *Hadîqa*, which is here presented, comprises a little more than one-sixth of the entire work. The subjects of which it treats may be briefly resumed as follows:--

After an introductory section in praise of God the author speaks of the impotence of reason for the attaining a knowledge of God; of God's Unity, of God as First Cause and Creator and delivers more than one attack against anthropomorphic conceptions of God (pp. 1-10). After speaking of the first steps of the ascent towards God, for which worldly wisdom is not a bad thing, with work and serenity (pp. 10-11), he devotes the next portion of the book to God as Provider, to His care for man through life, the uselessness of earthly possessions, and to God as guide on the road, but self must first be abandoned (pp. 11-46). A fine section on God's incomprehensibility to man might perhaps come more fittingly at an earlier stage instead of here (pp. 16-18). After overcoming self, God's special favour is granted to the traveller on the

---

[2] A Literary History of Persia, Vol. II., p. 319.

path: but we see crookedly, and He alone knows what is best for us: He has ordered all things well, and what seems evil is so only in appearance (pp. 18-25).

The greater part of the book is really concerned with the life and experiences of the Ṣūfī, and especially with continually repeated injunctions as to abandonment of the world and of self; to be dead to this world is to live in the other. Pp. 25-30 are thus concerned with poverty in this world, with loss of the, self, humility, man's insignificance and God's omnipotence; pp. 30-34 with the necessity of continual remembrance of God, of never living apart from Him, and again of dying to the world; death to the world leads to high position with God. There follows (pp. 34-41) a series of passages on the duty of thanksgiving for God's mercies; His mercy however has its counterpart in His anger, and examples of His wrath are given; then returning again to the subject of His mercies, the author speaks of God's omniscience, and His knowledge of the wants of His servants; we must therefore trust in God for all the necessaries of life, they will be given as long as life is destined to last. Two later pages (48-50), which are similarly devoted to the subject of trust in God, should probably come here. Pp. 41-48 deal with the Ṣūfīs desire for God, and his zeal in pursuing the path; various directions for the road are given, especially as rewards the abandonment of the world and of self, and fixing the desires on God only; union with God is the. goal. The abandonment of self is again the theme of pp. 50-51.

A portion of the book (pp. 51-56) is, curiously, here devoted to the interpretation of dreams; after which the author treats of the incompatibility of the two worlds, again of the abandonment of earth and self, and of the attainment of the utmost degree of annihilation (pp. 56-58). There follows a passage on the treatment of schoolboys, a comparison with the learner on the Ṣūfī path, and an exhortation to strive in pursuing it (pp. 58-60). The next portion of the book (pp., 60-67) treats of charity and gifts as a form of renunciation, of relinquishing riches for God's sake; prosperity is injurious to the soul, and the world must be abandoned; possessions and friends are useless, and each must trust to himself; each will find his deserts hereafter, and receive the reward of what he has worked for here.

Pp. 67-80 treat of prayer, the preparation for which consists in purity of heart, humility, and dependence upon God. Prayer must come from the heart; the believer must be entirely absorbed in his devotions. Prayer must be humble; the believer must come in poverty and perplexity, and only so can receive God's kindness. A number of addresses to God follow, prayers for help, and humble supplications to God on the part of the author. A few pages (80-92) treat of God's kindness in drawing men towards himself, though His ways may appear harsh at first. The progress of the believer is described in a strain of hyperbole (pp. 82-83); and this portion closes with a few sections (pp. 83-86) on God's majesty and omnipotence somewhat after the manner of those in the earlier part of the book.

In pp. 86-97 the author speaks of the Qur'ân, and its excellence and sweetness. The letter however is not the essential: its true meaning is not to be discovered by reason alone. The Qur'ân is often dishonoured, especially by theologians, and by professional readers, who read it carelessly and without understanding it. A short section (pp. 97-98) on humility and self-effacement follows, and the book is brought to a close by a description of the godlessness of the world before the advent of Muḥammad (pp. 98-100), which serves to introduce the subject of the Second Chapter.

Though it must he admitted that the author is occasionally obscure, sometimes dull, and not infrequently prosaic, some fine sections and a larger number of short passages of great beauty are contained in this chapter; I may perhaps be permitted especially to refer to the sections "In His Magnification," pp. 16-18. and "On Poverty and Perplexity," p. 74; while as characteristic and on the whole favourable passages may be mentioned "On His Omniscience, and His Knowledge of the Minds of Men," pp. 37-39; " On the Incompatibility of the Two Abodes," pp. 56-58; "On intimate Friendship and Attachment," pp. 62-63; and certain of the addresses to God contained in pp. 74-77.

# VI.--SANÂ'Î'S PREFACE.

The author's Preface to the work, given in A and L, and occupying in the latter nearly thirteen closely printed pages, is here given in abstract. It was not, as will appear, written specially as an introduction to the _Hadîqa_, but to his collected works.

After an opening section in praise of God, the author introduces the tradition, "_When a son of Adam dies, his activity ceases, except in three things; a permanent bequest, and knowledge by which men are benefited, and pious sons who invoke blessings on him after his death._" Considering these words one day, and reflecting that none of the three conditions was applicable to himself, he became sorrowful, and continued for some time in a state of grief and depression. one, day while in this condition, he was visited by his friend Aḥmad b. Mas`ûd, who inquired the cause of his sorrow. The author told him that, not fulfilling any one of the above conditions, he was afraid to die; possessing not one of these three advocates at court, he would stand without possessions or adornment in the Presence of the Unity. His friend then began to comfort him, saying, "First let me tell you a story." Sanâ'î replied, "Do so."

Aḥmad b. Mas`ûd then related how one day a company of women wished to have audience with Fâṭima, Muḥammad's daughter. Muḥammad gave permission; but Fâṭima, weeping, said, "O Father, how long is it since I have had even a little shawl for my head? and that mantle that I had pieced together in so many places with date-leaves is in pledge with Simeon the Jew. How can I receive them?" But Muḥammad said, "There is no help; you must go." Fâṭima went ashamed to the interview, and came back in sorrow to her father; who was comforting her when the rustle of Gabriel's wings was heard. Gabriel looked at Fâṭima and asked, "What is this sorrow? Ask the women, then, what garments they had on, and what thou." Muḥammad sent a messenger to the women, who returned, and said, "It was so, at the time when the Mistress of Creation bestowed beauty on that assembly, that the onlookers were astounded; though clothed, they seemed to themselves naked; and among themselves they were asking 'Whence came this fine linen, and from which shop this embroidery? What skilful artificers, what nimble-fingered craftsmen!'" Fâṭima said, "O my father, why didst thou not tell me, that I might have been glad?" He answered, "O dear one, thy beauty consisted in that which was concealed inside thyself."

"By my life," continued Aḥmad, "such modesty was allowable in Fâṭima, brought up in seclusion; but here we have a strong and able man of happy fortune, one who is known as a pattern to others in both practice and theory! Though thou hast considered thyself naked, yet they have clothed thee in a robe from the wardrobe of Eternity. Is it proper for this robe to be concealed,

35

instead of being displayed for the enlightenment of others? " And adverting to the saying, " *When a son of Adam dies, his work is cut short, except in three things,*" he takes the three one by one. First, *a continuing alms*; but '*Every kindness is an alms; and it is a kindness that thou meet thy brother with a cheerful countenance, and that thou empty thy bucket into the pots of thy brother*,' that is, alms does not wholly consist in spreading food before a glutton, or giving some worthless thing to a pauper; it is a truer alms and a more imperishable hospitality to wear a cheerful countenance before one's friends, " and if others have the outward semblance of alms, thou hast its inward essence; and if they have set forth a table of food before men, thou hast set forth a table of life before their souls; so much for what thou sayest, 'I am excluded from a continuing alms!'"

Ahmad b. Mas`ûd then takes up the second point, knowledge that benefits; and quotes, " *We take refuge with God from knowledge which does not benefit*" and "*Many a wise man is destroyed by his ignorance and his knowledge which does not advantage him.*" As examples of knowledge that does not benefit he takes the science of metaphysics, a science tied by the leg to desire and notoriety, lying under the opprobrium of "*He who learns the science of metaphysics is a heretic, and flys in circles in the air*," as well as of the saying "*A science newly born, weak in its credentials*"--"I have perfected it for the sake of heresy, and so peace." Then similarly the science of calculation, a veil which diverts attention from the Truth, a curtain in front of the subtilties of religion; and the science of the stars, a science of conjectures and the seed of irreligion, for " *Whoso credits a soothsayer has become an infidel.*" After a tirade against the ordinary type of learned man, he proceeds, "All their falsifyings and terrorizings and imaginings and conjecturings are limited by their own defects; that philosophy of the law is cherished which is notorious over all the quarters and regions of the world; there is your '*knowledge that men benefit by*'! From earth to Pleiades who is there sees any benefit in our doctors?" He then tells Sanâ'î that he is master of a more excellent wisdom; "*the poets are the chiefs of speech*;" "*the gift of the poets comes from the piety of the parents*;" "*verily from poetry comes wisdom*;" and will have none of such sayings as "*poetry is of the affairs of Satan.*"

As to the third part of the tradition, *and pious descendants to invoke blessings on him after his death*, Ahmad says, "The sons which suffice are thy sons; what son born in the way of generation and begetting is dearer than thy sons, or more honoured? Who has ever seen children like thine, all safe from the vicissitudes of time? The sons of poets are the poets' words, as a former master has said--

'A learned man never desires son or wife
Should the offspring of both these fail, the scholar's offspring would not
be cut off.'

A son according to the flesh may be a defilement to a family; but the son of
intelligence and wisdom is an ornament to the household. These sons of yours
you cannot disown."

He then asks Sanâ'î why he has thus become a recluse, and indolent and
languid. This languidness is indeed preferable to a total heedlessness and
forgetfulness of God, though Mutanabbi has said--

"*I have not seen anything of the faults of men like the failure of those
who are able to reach the end.*"

He asks Sanâ'î not to bring forward the saying, "*Laziness is sweeter than
honey,*" but to bestir himself and collect and complete his poetical works.

Sanâ'î tells us that he submitted himself to the advice of his friend, but brought
forward the difficulties of house and food, since the work could not be
performed friendless and homeless. Aḥmad b. Mas`ûd thereupon built him a
house, gave him an allowance for his maintenance for one year, and sent also a
supply of clothing. He was therefore enabled to complete and arrange his
writing's free from all care and anxiety. The preface ends with the praise of his
generous friend.

### The First Book of the Ḥadîqatu'-l-Ḥaqîqat of Sanâ'î.

IN THE NAME OF GOD, THE MERCIFUL, THE COMPASSIONATE.

O Thou who nurturest the mind, who adornest the body, O Thou who givest
wisdom, who showest mercy on the foolish, Creator and Sustainer of earth and
time, Guardian and Defender of dweller and dwelling; dwelling and dweller, all
is of Thy creation; time and earth, all is under Thy command; fire and wind,
water and the firm ground, all are under the control of Thy omnipotence, O
Thou the Ineffable. From thy throne to earth, all is but a particle of what
Thou hast created; the living intelligence is Thy swift messenger. Every tongue
that moves within the mouth possesses life for the purpose of praising Thee;
Thy great and sacred names are a proof of Thy bounty and beneficence and
mercy. Each one of them is greater than heaven and earth and angel; they are a
thousand and one, and they are ninety-nine; each one of them is related to one
of man's needs, but those who are not in Thy secrets are excluded from them.

O Lord, of thy grace and pity admit this heart and soul to a sight of Thy name!

Infidelity and faith, both travelling on Thy road, exclaim, He is alone, He has no partner. The Creator, the Bounteous, the Powerful is He; the One, the Omnipotent,--not like unto us is He, the Living, the Eternal, the All-knowing, the Potent, the Feeder of creation, the Conqueror and the Pardoner. He causes movement, and causes rest; He it is who is alone, and ha; no partner; to whatever thing thou ascribest fundamental existence, that thou assertest to be His partner; beware!

Our weakness is a demonstration of His perfection; His omnipotence is the deputy of His names. Both *No* and *He* returned from that mansion of felicity with pocket and purse empty. What is there above imagination, and reason, and perception, and thought, except the mind of him who knows God? for to a knower of God, wherever he is, in whatever state, the throne of God is as a carpet under his shoe. The seeing soul knows praise is folly, if given to other than the Creator; He who from earth can create the body, and make the wind the register of speech, the Giver of reason, the Inspirer of hearts, who calls forth the soul, the Creator of causes;--generation and corruption, all is his work; He is the source of all creation, and the place to which it returns all comes from Him and all returns to Him; good and evil all proceeds to Him. He creates the freewill of the good and of the wicked; He is the Author of the soul, the Originator of wisdom; He from nothing created thee something; thou wert of no account, and He exalted thee.

No mind can reach a comprehension of His mode of being; the reason and soul know not His perfection. The mind of Intelligence is dazzled by His majesty, the soul's eye is blinded before His perfection. The Primal Intelligence is a product of His nature,--it He admitted to a knowledge of himself. Imagination lags before the glory of His essence; understanding moves confined before His nature's mode of being. His fire, which in haughtiness He made His carpet, burnt the wing of reason; the soul is a serving-man in His pageant, reason a novitiate in His school. What is reason in this guest-house? only a crooked writer of the script of God.

What of this intelligence, agitator of trifles? What of this changing inconstant nature?, When He shows to intelligence the road to Himself, then only can intelligence fitly praise Him. Since Intelligence was the first of created things, Intelligence is above all choicest things besides; yet Intelligence is but one word out of His record, the Soul one of the foot-soldiers at His door. Love He perfected through a reciprocal love; but intelligence He tethered even by intelligence. Intelligence, like us, is bewildered on the road to His nature, like us confounded. He is intelligence of intelligence, and soul of soul; and what is above that, that He is. How through the promptings of reason and soul and senses can one come to know God? But that God showed him the way, how could man ever have become acquainted with Divinity?

## ON THE KNOWLEDGE OF GOD.

Of himself no one can know Him; His nature can only be known through Himself. Reason sought His truth,--it ran not well; impotence hastened on His road, and knew Him. His mercy said, Know me; otherwise who, by reason and sense, could know Him? How is it possible by the guidance of the senses? How can a nut rest firmly on the summit of a dome? Reason will guide thee, but only to the door; His grace must carry thee to Himself. Thou canst not journey there by reason's guidance; perverse like others, commit not thou this folly. His grace leads us on the road; His works are guide and witness to Him. O thou, who art incompetent to know thine own nature, how wilt thou ever know God? Since thou art incapable of knowing thyself, how wilt thou become a knower of the Omnipotent? Since thou art unacquainted with the first steps towards a knowledge of Him, how thinkest thou to conceive of Him as He is?

In describing Him in argument, speech is a comparison, and silence a dereliction of duty. Reason's highest attainment on His road is amazement; the people's riches is their zeal for Him.

Imagination falls short of His attributes; understanding vainly boasts her powers; the prophets are confounded at these sayings, the saints stupefied at these attributes. He is the desired and lord of reason and soul, the goal of disciple and devotee. Reason is as a guide to His existence; all other existences are under the foot of His existence. His acts are not bounded by 'inside' and 'outside'; His essence is superior to 'how' and 'why.' Intelligence has not reached the comprehension of His essence; the soul and heart of reason are dust upon this road; reason, without the collyrium of friendship with Him, has no knowledge of His divinity. Why dost thou instigate imagination to discuss Him? How shall a raw youth speak of the Eternal?

By reason and thought and sense no living thing can come to know God. When the glory of His nature manifests itself to reason, it sweeps away both reason and soul. Let reason be invested with dignity in the rank where stands the faithful Gabriel; yet before all His majesty a Gabriel becomes less than a sparrow through awe; reason arriving there bows down her head, the soul flying there folds her wing. The raw youth discusses the Eternal only in the light of his shallow sense and wicked soul; shall thy nature, journeying towards the majesty and glory of His essence, attain to a knowledge of Him?

# ON THE ASSERTION OF THE UNITY.

He is One, and number has no place in Him; He is Absolute, and dependence is far removed from Him; not that One which reason and understanding can know, not that Absolute which sense and imagination can recognise. He is not multitude, nor paucity; one multiplied by one remains one. In duality is only evil and error; in singleness is never any fault.

While multitude and confusion remain in thy heart, say thou 'One' or 'Two,'-- what matter, for both are the same. Thou, the devil's pasture, know for certain what, and how much, and why, and how! Have a care! His greatness comes not from multitude; His essence is above number and quality; the weak searcher may not ask '*Is it*' or '*Who*' concerning Him. No one has uttered the attributes of the Creator, HE,--quantity, quality, why, or what, who, and where. His hand is power, His face eternity; 'to come' is His wisdom, 'the descent' His gift; His two feet are the majesty of vengeance and dignity, His two fingers are the effective power of His command and will. All existences are subject to His omnipotence; all are present to Him, all seek Him; the motion of light is towards light-how can light be separated from the sun?

In comparison with His existence eternity began but the day before yesterday; it came at dawn, but yet came late. How can His working be bounded by eternity? Eternity without beginning is a houseborn slave of his; and think not nor imagine that eternity without end (is more), for eternity without end is like to eternity without beginning.

How shall He have a place, in size greater or smaller? for place itself has no place. How shall there be a place for the Creator of place, a heaven for the Maker of heaven himself? Place cannot attain to Him, nor time; narration can give no information of Him, nor observation. Not through columns is His state durable; His nature's being has its place in no habitation.

O thou, who art in bondage to form and delineation, bound by '*He sat upon the throne*'; form exists not apart from contingencies, and accords not with the majesty of the Eternal. Inasmuch as He was sculptor, He was not image; '*He sat*' was, not throne, nor earth. Continue calling '*He sat*' from thy inmost soul, but think not His essence is bound by dimensions; for '*He sat*' is a verse of the Qur'ân, and to say '*He has no place*' is an article of faith. The throne is like a ring outside a door; it knows not the attributes of Godhead. The word 'speech' is written in the Book; but shape and voice and form are far from Him; '*God descends*' is written in tradition, but believe not thou that He comes and goes; the throne is mentioned in order to exalt it, the reference to the Ka`ba is to glorify it. To say '*He has no place*' is the gist of religion; shake thy head, for it is a fitting opportunity for praise. They pursue Ḥusain with enmity because 'Alî spoke the word '*He has no place.*'

He made an earth for His creation in this form; behold how He has made a nest for thee! Yesterday the sky was not, to-day it is; again to-morrow it will not be,--yet He remains. He will fold up the veil of smoke in front of Him;-- '*On a day we will fold up the heavens;*' (Qur. 21:103) breathe thou forth a groan. When the knowers of God live in Him, the Eternal, they cleave '*behold*' and '*He*' in two through the middle.

# ON GOD AS FIRST CAUSE.

The course of time is not the mould whence issues His eternal duration, nor temperament the cause of His beneficence; without His word, time and temperament exist not, as apart from His favour the soul enters not the body. This and that both are wanting and worthless; that and this both are foolish and impotent. 'Old' and 'new' are words inapplicable to His essence; He is, for He consists not of any existences except Himself. His kingdom cannot be known to its limits, His nature cannot be described even to its beginning; His acts and His nature are beyond instrument and direction, for His Being is above '*Be*' and '*He*'.

Before thou wert in existence a greater than thou for thy sake brought together the causes that went to form thee; in one place under the heavens by the command and act of God were the four temperaments prepared; I their gathering together is a proof of His power; His power is the draughtsman of His wisdom. He who laid down the plan of thee without pen can also complete it without colours; within thee, not in yellow and white and red and black, God has pourtrayed His work; and without thee He has designed the spheres; of what?--of wind and water and fire and earth. The heavens will not for ever leave to thee thy colours,--yellow and black and red and white; the spheres take back again their gifts, but the print of God remains for ever; He who without colours drew thy outlines will never take back from thee thy soul. By His creative power He brought thee under an obligation, for His grace has made thee an instrument I of expression of Himself; He said, 'I was a hidden treasure; creation was created that thou mightest know me; the eye like to a precious pearl through *kâf* and *nûn* He made a mouth filled with Yâ în.

Sew no purse and tear not thy veil; lick no plate and buy not blandishment. All things are contraries, but by the command of God all travel together on the same road; in the house of non-existence the plan of all is laid down for all eternity by the command of the Eternal; four essences, through the exertion of the seven stars, become the means of bodying forth the plan. Say, The world of evil and of good proceeds not except from Him and to Him, nay, is Himself. All objects receive their outline and forms from Him, their material basis as well as their final shape. Element and material substance, the form and colours clothing the four elements,--all things know as limited and finite, as but a ladder for thy ascent to God.

## ON PURITY OF HEART.

Then, since the object of desire exists not in anyplace, how canst thou purpose to journey towards Him on foot? The highroad by which thy spirit and prayers can travel towards God lies in the polishing of the mirror of the heart. The mirror of the heart becomes not free from the rust of infidelity and hypocrisy by opposition and hostility; the burnisher of the mirror is your steadfast faith; again, what is it? It is the unsullied purity of your religion. To him in whose heart is no confusion the mirror and the form imaged will not appear as the same thing; although in form thou art in the mirror, that which is in the mirror is not thou,--thou art one, as the mirror is another. The mirror knows nothing of thy form; it and thy form are very different things; the mirror receives the image by means of light, and light is not to be separated from the sun;--the fault, then, is in the mirror and the eye.

Whoso remains for ever behind a veil, his likeness is as the owl and the sun.. If the owl is incapacitated by the sun, it is because of its own weakness, not because of the sun, the light of the sun is spread throughout the world, the misfortune comes from the weakness of the bat's eye.

Thou seest not except by fancy and sense, for thou dost not even know the line, the surface and the point; thou stumblest on this road of knowledge, and for months and years remainest tarrying in discussion; but in this matter he utters only folly who does not know the manifestation of God through his incarnation in man. If thou wishest that the mirror should reflect the face, hold it not crooked and keep it bright; for the sun, though not niggardly of his light, seen in a mist looks only like glass, and a Yûsuf more beautiful than an angel seems in a dagger to have a devil's face. Thy dagger will not distinguish truth from falsehood; it will not serve thee as a mirror. Thou canst better see thy image in the mirror of thy heart than in thy clay; break loose from the chain thou hast fettered thyself with,--for thou wilt be free when thou hast got clear from thy clay; since clay is dark and heart is bright, thy clay is a dustbin and thy heart a rose-garden. Whatever increases the brightness of thy heart brings nearer God's manifestation of Himself to thee; because Abû Bakr's purity of heart was greater than others', he was favoured by a special manifestation.

# ON THE BLIND MEN AND THE AFFAIR OF THE ELEPHANT.

There was a great city in the country of G͟hûr, in which all the people were blind. A certain king passed by that place, bringing his army and pitching his camp on the plain. He had a large and magnificent elephant to minister to his pomp and excite awe, and to attack in battle. A desire arose among the people to see this monstrous elephant, and a number of the blind, like fools, visited it, every one running in his haste to find out its shape and form. They came, and being without the sight of their eyes groped about it with their hands; each of them by touching one member obtained a notion of some one part; each one got a conception of an impossible object, and fully believed his fancy true. When they returned to the people of the city, the others gathered round them, all expectant, so misguided and deluded were they. They asked about the appearance and shape of the elephant, and what they told all listened to. One asked him whose hand had come upon its ear about the elephant; he said, It is a huge and formidable object, broad and rough and spreading, like a carpet. And he whose hand had come upon its trunk said, I have found out about it; it is straight and hollow in the middle like a pipe, a terrible thing and an instrument of destruction. And he who had felt the thick hard legs of the elephant said, As I have it in mind, its form is straight like a planed pillar. Every one had seen some one of its parts, and all had seen it wrongly. No mind knew the whole,--knowledge is never the companion of the blind all, like fools deceived, fancied absurdities.

Men know not the Divine essence; into this subject the philosophers may not enter.

## ON THE ABOVE ALLEGORY.

One talks of 'the foot', the other of 'the hand', pushing beyond all limits their foolish words; that other speaks of 'fingers' and 'change of place' and 'descending', and of His coming as an incarnation. Another considers in his science His 'settling himself' and 'throne' and 'couch', and in his folly speaks of 'He sat' and 'He reclined', making of his foolish fancy a bell to tie round his neck. 'His face' says one; 'His feet' another; and no one says to him, 'Where is thy object?' From all this talk there comes altercation, and there results what happened in the case of the blind men and the elephant.

Exalted be the name of Him who is exempt from 'what' and 'how'! the livers of the prophets have become blood. Reason hamstringed by this saying; the sciences of the learned are folded up. All have come to acknowledge their weakness; woe to him who persists in his folly! Say, It is allegorical; depend not on it, and fly from foolish conceptions. The text of the Qur'ân--we believe it all; and the traditions--we admit the whole of them.

## OF THOSE WHO HEED NOT.

A discerning man questioned one of the indifferent, whom he saw to be very foolish and thoughtless, saying, Hast thou ever seen saffron, or hast thou only heard the name? He said, I have it by me, and have eaten a good deal of it, not once only, but a hundred times and more. Said the wise and discerning man to him, Bravo, wretch! Well done, my friend! Thou knowest not that there is a bulb as well! How long wilt thou wag thy beard in thy folly?

He who knows not his own soul, how shall he know the soul of another? and he who only knows hand and foot, how shall he know the Godhead? The prophets are unequal to understanding this matter; why dost thou foolishly claim to do so? When thou hast brought forward a demonstration of this subject, then thou wilt know the pure essence of the faith; otherwise what have faith and thou in common? thou hadst best be silent, and speak not folly. The learned talk nonsense all; for true religion is not woven about the feet of everyone.

## ON THE STEPS OF ASCENT.

Make not thy soul's nest in hell, nor thy mind's lodging in deception; wander not in the neighbourhood of foolishness and absurdities, nor by the door of the house of vain imagining. Abandon vain conceits, that thou mayest find admission to that court; for that mansion of eternity is for thee, and this abode of mortality is not thy place; for thee is that mansion of eternity prepared,-- abandon to-day, and give up thy life for to-morrow's sake. This world's evil and good, its deceit and truth, are only for the ignoble among the sons of Adam.

To a high roof the steps are many,--why art thou contented with one step? The first step towards it is serenity, according to the attestation of the lord of knowledge; and after it thou comest to the second step,--the wisdom of life, of form and matter.

Know thou the truth,--that there is not in the world for the offspring of Adam a better staircase to mount the eternal heaven by, than wisdom and work. The wisdom of life makes strong the mind for both the upper and the lower abode; strive thou in this path, and although thou do not so in that, yet thou shalt not do amiss. Whoso sows the seed of sloth, sloth will bring him impiety for fruit; whoso took unto himself folly and sloth, his legs lost their power and his work failed I know nothing worse than sloth; it turns Rustams into cowards. Thou wert created for work, and a robe of honour is ready cut for thee; why are thou content with tatters? Why wilt thou not desire those striped garments of Arabia? Whence wilt thou get fortune and kingdom when thou art idle sixty days a month? Idleness in the day, and ease at night,--thou wilt hardly reach the throne of the Sasanians. Know that handle of club and hilt of sword are crown and throne to kings who know not the moisture of weeping eyes; but he who wanders about after money and a meal cringes ignoble and vile before a clenched fist.

Possessing knowledge, possess also serenity like the mountain; be not distressed at the disasters of fortune. Knowledge without serenity is an unlighted candle, both together are like the bee's honey; honey without wax typifies the noble, wax without honey is only for burning.

Abandon this abode of generation and corruption; leave the pit, and make for thy destined home; for on this dry heap of dust is a mirage, and fire appears as water. The man of pure heart unites the two worlds in one; the lover makes but one out of all three abodes.

## ON THE PROTECTION AND GUARDIANSHIP OF GOD.

Whoso is fenced around by divine aid, a spider spreads its web before him; a lizard utters his praise, a serpent seeks to please him. His shoe treads the summit of the throne; his ruby lip is the world's fitting ornament; in his mouth poison becomes sugar; in his hand a stone becomes a jewel. Whoso lays his head on this threshold places his foot on the head of things temporal; wise reason is powerless to explain these things, for all are powerless who come not to this door. I fear that through thy ignorance and folly thou wilt one day be left helpless on _Sirât_; thy ignorance will deliver thee to the fire; see how it is administering the soporific lettuce and poppies to thee.

Thou hast seen how in the middle of a morsel of food that one eats there will appear a grain of wheat, which has survived the attack of locust, and bird, and beast, has seen the heat of heaven and the glow of the oven, and remained unchanged under thy millstone. Who preserved it? God, God. He is a sufficient protector for thee,--for possessions and life and breath; thou art of His creation, that is enough. If thou procurest dog and chain thou canst overcome the antelope of the desert, and in thy trust and sincere belief in this thou art free from anxiety as regards a maintenance and livelihood: I say to thee,--and with reason and judgment, so that thou mayst not shut the door of thine ear against my words,--Thy trust in dog and chain I see is greater than in the All-hearing and All-seeing; the light of thy faith, if standing on this foundation, is given over to destruction by a dog and a thing of iron.

## THE PARABLE OF THOSE WHO GIVE ALMS.

A certain wise and liberal man gave away so many bags of gold before his son's eyes that when he saw his father's munificence he broke forth into censure and remonstrance, saying, Father, where is my share of this? He said, O son, in the treasury of God; I have given to God thy portion, leaving no executor and none to divide it with thee, and He will give it thee again.

He is Himself our Provider and our Master; shall He not suffice us, both for faith and worldly goods? He is no other than the disposer of our lives; He will not oppress thee,--He is not of those. To everyone He gives back seventy-fold; and if He closes one door against thee, He opens ten.

## ON THE CAUSE OF OUR MAINTENANCE.

Seest thou not that before the beginning of thy existence God the All-wise, the Ineffable, when He had created thee in the womb gave thee of blood thy sustenance for nine months? Thy mother nourished thee in her womb, then after nine months brought thee forth; that door of support He quickly closed on thee, and bestowed on thee two better doors, for He then acquainted thee with the breast,--two fountains running for thee day and night; He said, Drink of these both; eat and welcome, for it is not forbidden thee. When after two years she weaned thee, all became changed for thee; He gave thee thy sustenance by means of thy two hands and feet,--'Take it by means of these, and by those go where thou wilt! ' If He closed the two doors against thee, it is but Light, for instead of two, four doors have appeared,--'Take by means of these, by those go on to victory; go seek thy daily bread throughout the world!' When suddenly there comes on thee thy appointed time, and the things of the world all pass away, and the two hands and feet fail in their office, to thee in thy helpless state He gives an exchange for these four. Hands and feet are shut up in the tomb, and eight heavens become thy fortune; eight doors are opened to thee, the virgins and youths of Paradise come before thee, that going joyfully to any door thou wilt thou mayest lose remembrance of this world.

O youth, hear this saying, and despair not of God's bounty. If God has given thee knowledge of Himself and put belief within thy heart, the robe of honour which is to thee like thy wedding-garment He will not take from thee on the day of resurrection. If thou hast neither learning nor gold, yet hast this, thou wilt not be destitute. He will bring thee to glory,--thou shalt not be disgraced; He will set thee in honour,--thou shalt not be despised. Thy possessions,--give not thy soul to their keeping; what He has given thee, hold thou fast to that. Thou layest up treasure,--thou shalt not see it again; if thou gavest it to Him, He would give it thee again. Thou puttest gold in the fire,--it burns up the dross, so He burns thy pure gold; when He has burnt out the bad, the good He gives to thee; fortune bends down her head to thee from the skies. The more enduring the benefit afforded by the fire, the kinder on that account is He who kindles the fire; thou knowest not what is good nor what bad; He is a better treasurer for thee than thou for thyself. A friend is a serpent; why seekest thou his door? the serpent is thy friend; why fliest thou from it in terror?

O seeker of the shell of the pearl of '*Unless*', lay down clothing and life on the shore of '*Not*'; God's existence inclines only towards him who has ceased to exist; non-existence is the necessary provision for the journey. Till in annihilation thou lay aside thy cap thou wilt not set thy face on the road to eternal life; when thou becomest nothing, thou runnest towards God; the path of mendicancy leads up to Him. If fortune crushes thee down, *the most excellent of Creators* will restore thee. Rise, and have done with false fables; *forsake* thy ignoble passions, *and come hither.*

## OF THE RIGHT GUIDANCE

Every indication of the road thou receivest, O darwîsh, count it a gift of God, not thine own doing; He is the cause of the bestowal of benefits, He it is to whom the soul is guided, and He its guide. Recognise that it is God's favour guides thee on the path of duty and religion and His ordinance, not thine own strength. He is the giver of the light of truth and instruction, both Guardian of the world and its Observer too. He is kinder than mother and father; He it is who shall guide thee to Paradise.

Because of the unbelief of the people He made us our religion; He made us see clearly in the darkness. See the favour of God the Guider! for out of all creation He made man His chosen. His majesty needs not saint nor prophet for the enlightening of male or female; for the guidance of the six princes He made a cat a prophet, a dog a saint. Whose comes to Him and lends his ear, comes not of himself, but His grace leads him; His grace will guide thee to the end, and then the heavens will be thy slave. Know that it is He who makes the soul prostrate itself, as even through the sun the clouds give bounteous rain.

# ON THE SURRENDER OF THE SELF.

Dost thou desire thy collar of lace to be washed, then first give thy coat to the fuller. Strip off thy coat, for on the road to the King's gate there are many to tear it. At the first step that Adam took, the wolf of affliction tore his coat: when Cain became athirst to oppress, did not Abel give up his coat and die? Was it not when Idrîs threw off his coat that he saw the door of Paradise open to him? When the Friend of God remorselessly tore their garments from star and moon and sun, his night became bright as day, and the fire of Nimrod became a garden and a rose-bower. Look at Solomon, who in his justice gave the coat of his hope to the fuller; jinn and men, birds and ants and locusts, in the depth of the: waters of the Red Sea, on the tips of the branches, all raised their face to him, all became subservient to his command; when the lustre of his nature had been burnt in the fire of his soul, the heavens laid his body on the back of the wind.

When the venerable Moses, reared in sorrow, turned his face in grief and pain towards Midian, in bodily labour he tore off the coat from his anguished heart. For ten years he served Shu`aib, till the door of the invisible was opened to his soul. His hand became bright as his piercing eye; he became the crown on the head of the men of Sinai.

When the Spirit, drawing breath from the spiritual ocean, had received the grace of the Lord, he sent his coat to the cleanser of hearts at the first stage of his journey. He gave brightness to his soul, He gave him kingship, even in childhood. By the Eternal Power, through encouragement in secret and grace made manifest, he lost the self; the leprous body became dark again through him as the shadow on the earth, the blind eye became bright as the steps of the throne. Whoso like him seeks neither name nor reputation, can produce ten kinds (of food) from one jar. A stone with him became fragrant as musk; the dead rose to living action and spoke. By his grace life broke forth in the dead earth of the heart; by his power he animated the heart of the mire.

When predestined fate had closed the shops, and the hand of God's decree lay in the hollow of non-existence, the world was full of evil passions, the market full of ruffians and patrols. Then He sent a vicegerent into this world to abolish oppression; when he appeared from mid-heaven, fervid in soul and pure in body, he wore no coat on the religious path; then what could he give to the fullers of the land? When he passed from this mortal state to eternal life he became the ornament and glory of this perishable world.

## IN HIS MAGNIFICATION.

When He shows His Nature to His creation, into what mirror shall He enter? The burden of proclaiming the Unity not everyone bears; the desire of proclaiming the Unity not everyone tastes. In every dwelling is God adored; but the Adored cannot be circumscribed by any dwelling. The earthly man, accompanied by unbelief and anthropomorphism, wanders from the road; on the road of truth thou must abandon thy passions;-rise., and forsake this vile sensual nature; when thou hast come forth from Abode and Life, then, through God, thou wilt see God.

How shall this sluggish body worship Him, or how can Life and Soul know Him? A ruby of the mine is but a pebble there; the soul's wisdom talks but folly there. Speechlessness is praise,--enough of thy speech; babbling will be but sorrow and harm to thee,--have done!

His Nature, to one who knows Him and is truly learned, is above '*How*' and '*What*' and '*Is it not*' and '*Why*.' His creative power is manifest, the justice of His wisdom; His wrath is secret, the artifice of His majesty. A form of water and earth is dazzled by His love, the eye and heart are blinded by His Nature. Reason in her uncleanness, wishing to see Him, says, like Moses, '*Show me*'; when the messenger comes forth from that glory, she says in its ear, '*I turn repentant unto thee*.' (Qur. 7:138 sq.) Discover then the nature of His Being through thy understanding! recite his thousand and one pure names. It is not fitting that His Nature should be covered by our knowledge; whatever thou hast heard, that is not He. 'Point' and 'line' and 'surface' in relation to His Nature are as if one should talk of His 'substance' and 'distance' and 'six surfaces'; the Author of those three is beyond place the Creator of these three is not contained in time. No philosopher knows of imperfection in Him, while He knows the secrets of the invisible world; He is acquainted with the recesses of the mind, and the secrets of which as yet there has been formed no sketch upon thy heart.

*Kâf* and *nûn* are only letters that we write, but what is *kun*? the hurrying of the agent of the divine decree. If He delays, or acts quickly, it depends not on His weakness; whether He is angry or placable depends not on His hate. His causation is known to neither infidelity nor faith, and neither is acquainted with His Nature. He is pure of those attributes the foolish speak of, purer than the wise can tell.

Reason is made up of confusion and conjecture, both limping over the earth's face. Conjecture and cogitation are no good guides; wherever conjecture and cogitation are, He is not. Conjecture and cogitation are of His creation; man and reason are His newly ripening plants. Since any affirmation about His Nature is beyond man's province, it is like a statement about his mother by a blind man; the blind man knows he has a mother, but what she is like he cannot imagine; his imagination is without any conception of what things are like, of ugliness and beauty, of inside and outside.

In a world of double aspect such as this, it would be wrong that thou shouldst be He, and He thou. If thou assert Him not, it is not well; if thou assert Him, it is thyself thou assertest, not He. If thou know not (that He is) thou art without religion, and if thou assert Him thou art of those who liken Him. Since He is beyond 'where' and 'when', how can He become a corner of thy thought? When the wayfarers travel towards Him, they vainly exclaim, 'Behold, Behold!' Men of hawk-like boldness are as ringdoves in the street, a collar on their necks, uttering 'Where, Where?'

If thou wilt, take hope, or if thou wilt, then fear; the All-wise has created nothing in vain. He knows all that has been done or will be done: thou knowest not,--yet know that He will assuage thy pain. In the knowledge of Him is naught better than submission, that so thou mayest learn His wisdom and His clemency. Of His wisdom He has given resources to His creatures, the greater to him who has the greater need; to all He has given fitting resources, for acquiring profit and warding off injury. What has gone, what comes, and what exists in the world, in such wise it was necessary; bring not folly into thy conversation; look thou with acceptance on His decrees.

## ON THE EARNEST STRIVING.

When thou hast passed from Self to being naught, gird up the loins of thy soul and set forth on the road, when thou standest up with loins girt thou hast placed a crown on thy soul's head. Set then the crown of the advance on the head of thy soul; let the foot that would retreat be the companion of the mire; though the thoughtless man laughs at this act, yet the wise chooses no other course.

Whoso turns not his face towards God, all his knowledge and possessions deem thou an idol. Who turns away his face from God's presence, in truth I call not him a man; a dog is better than a worthless man who turns away his face, for a dog finds not its prey without a search. A dog that lives in ease, though it gets fat, is not therefore more useful than a greyhound. He will not take hypocrisy and deceit and lying, but looks to a man's belief in the Unity and his sincerity. The eye that is fixed on wisdom chooses the Truth; the pleasure-regarding eye sees not the Truth. False is what delights the eye; the Truth enters not among earthy thoughts. Infidelity and faith both have their origin in thy hypocritical heart; the path is long because thy foot delays: were it not so, the road to Him is but one step,--be a slave, and thou becomest a king with Him. Know that the different names of the colours are illusory, that thy sustenance is to be sought in the river of the Absolute. Leave off thy talk, and come to the pavilion; loose thy heavy bonds from off thyself. Perhaps thou hast not tasted the true faith, hast not seen the face of truth and sincerity; so that thou thoughtest the mystery was plain to be seen, and things thou sawest plainly have been mysteries to thee. I see in thee no rightness of belief; if there were I would be the true dawn of religion to thee;--I would have made the path of the true faith plain to thee hadst thou not been a fool and a madman.

## OF THE TRAVELLER ON THE PATH.

A man should be like Abraham, that, through God, his shadow may become a shady place; in fear of him and by his teaching the universe dares to breathe; Pharaoh is destroyed by the mighty aid of a Moses whom God assists.

To the wayfarer towards God on the path of love His cheek is the dawn of morning; (who but He can tear away the veil by day, or hang the veil by night?) His mind is snatched away from bonds of earth; the spiritual rule of the world is made manifest to him. He treads the Throne under his feet like a carpet; he is an owl, but bears with him a phœnix. He becomes lord of this abode and that, the loyal slave of God; the pure Intelligence reveals its face to man, and beautifies his body with its own light. The bounty of God throws its shade over his heart; then he says, 'How He prolongs the shadow.' (Qur. 25:47) When his soul feels the touch of God, 'We make the sun' reveals its face to him (Qur. 25:48). The dumb all find tongues when they receive the perfume of life from his soul.

In His path the lovers recite to their souls the verse 'Every creature on the earth is subject to decay;' (Qur. 55:26) the heavens, and the natural world and its varied colours seem vile to his perception. Whoso is turned away from this wine, for him all its fragrance and colour is destroyed; so that when with new ear thou shalt hear the shouts of 'He is One, He has no partner,' thou shalt no longer in madness desire the varied colours, even though thy Jesus be the dyer. Thou shalt take what thou wilt of the colours, put them into one jar, and bring them out again;-listen truly, and not in folly: this saying is not for fools;-all these deceitful colours the jar of the Unity makes one colour. Then being now of one colour, all has become Him; the rope becomes slender when reduced to a single strand.

## ON BEING SILENT.

The path of religion is neither in works nor words; there are no buildings thereon, but only desolation. Whoso becomes silent to pursue the path, his speech is life and sweetness; if he speaks, it will not be out of ignorance, and if he is silent, it will not be from sloth; when silent, he is not devising frivolity; when speaking, he scatters abroad no trifling talk.

Those fools, the thieves and pickpockets, keep their knowledge to use in highway robbery. Thou seest, O Master, thou of many words, that thou hadst better have light in thy heart than words; when thou becomest silent, thou art most eloquent, but if thou speakest, thou art like a captain of war. '*Kun*,' consists of two letters, both voiceless; '*Hû*' consists of two letters, both silent. Doubt not concerning these words of mine; open thine eyes, pay heed for a little.

There exists the dog, and the stone; the stove of the bath, and the slave; but thou art excellent, like a jewel inside a casket. The king uses his silver for his daily needs, but his ruby be keeps for his treasure-house; silver is evil in its own ill-starred nature, the ruby is joyous because it is full of blood within.

The family of Barmak became great through their liberality; they were, so to say, close companions of generosity. Though fate pronounced their destruction, their name endures, indestructible as the spirit. The people of this generation, though amiable, are impudent as flies and wanton; in word they are all sweet as sugar, but when it comes to generosity, they tear men's hearts and burn their souls.

When He had adorned thy soul within thee, He held up before thee the mirror of the light; till pride made thee quick to anger, and thou lookedst upon thyself with the evil eye.

He has balanced day and night by the ruler of his justice, not by chance or at random.

While Reason digs for the secret, thou hast reached thy goal on the plain of Love.

The heart and soul of the seeker after God are concealed, but his tongue proclaims in truth, '*I am God.*'

## THE PARABLE OF THOSE WHO HEED NOT.

A fool saw a camel grazing, and said, Why is thy form all crooked? Said the camel, In disputing thus thou censurest the sculptor; beware! Look not on my crookedness in disparagement, and kindly take the straight road away from me. My form is thus because it is best so, as from a bow's being bent comes its excellence. Begone hence with thy impertinent interference, an ass's ear goes well with an ass's head.

The arch of the eyebrow, though it displease thee, is yet a fiting cupola over the eye; by reason of the eyebrow, the eye is able to look at the sun, and in virtue of the bloom of its strength becomes an adornment to the face. Evil and good, in the estimation of the wise, are both exceeding good; from Him there comes no evil; whatever thou seest to come from Him, though evil, it were well thou look on it all as good. To the body there comes its portion of ease and of pain; to the soul ease is as a treasure secured; but a twisted snake is over it, the hand and foot of Wisdom are at its side.

## THE PARABLE OF THE EYE OF THE SQUINT-EYED.

A squint-eyed son asked his father, O thou whose words are as a key to the things that are locked up, why saidst thou that a squinter sees double? I see no more things than there are; if a squint-eyed person counted things crookedly, the two moons that are in the heavens would seem four.

But he who spoke thus spoke in error; for if a squinter looks at a dome, it is doubled.

I fear that on the high-road of the faith thou art like the crooked-seeing squinter, or like the fool who senselessly quarrelled with the camel because of God's handiwork. His flawless creation is the *qibla* of our understanding; His changeless nature is the *ka 'ba* of our desire. He has exalted the soul in giving it wisdom; He has nourished His pardoning mercy on our faults. God well knows your turning to Him; His wisdom it is which prevents His answering your prayers. Though the physician hears his patient when he begs, he does not give earth to an earth-eater; and though his soul desire it, how shall He give earth through all his life to him who digs the earth? How shall His act be without a reason, or His decrees in accordance with thy weak understanding?

There are exceeding many who have drunk the cup of pure poison and have not died of it; nay, it is life's food to him who from the violence of his disease is wasted to a reed. In His wisdom and justice He has given to all more than all that is requisite; if the gnat bites the elephant's hide, tell him to flap his ears,-- he has a gnat dispeller in them; if there is a louse, thou hast a finger-nail; punish the flea, when it jumps on thee; though the mountains were full of snakes, fear not,--there are stones and an antidote on the mountain too; and if thou art apprehensive of the scorpion, thou hast slipper and shoe for it. If pain abounds in the world, everyone has a thousand remedies.

In accordance with his scheme He has suspended together the sphere of intense cold and the globe of fire. The motions of the body are rendered equable, the coolness of the brain and the warmth of the heart are both moderated; the liver and heart, by means of the stomach and arteries, send forth water and air to the body, that through breath and blood the heart by its movement, and the liver by its quiescence, may give the body life.

There is a spiritual kingdom in the universe, and also a temporal power; above the throne light, and below darkness; both these principles He bestowed at the creation, when He spread His shadow over His handiwork. The temporal world He has given of His bounty to the body, the spiritual world as a glory to the soul; that so both inner and outer man may receive food, the body from the lord of this world, the soul from the Lord of the spirit-world; for through all His creation God keeps a benign grace for the benefit of the noble soul.

The acute thinker knows that what He does is well; it is thou who namest some things evil and some good, otherwise all that comes from Him is pure kindness. Evil comes not into existence from Him; how can evil subsist with Godhead? Only the foolish and ignorant do evil; the Doer of good Himself does no evil. If He gives poison, deem it sweet; if He shows wrath, deem it mercy. Good is the cupping-glass our mothers apply to us, and good too the dates they give.

## AGAIN THE PARABLE OF THOSE WHO HEED NOT.

Dost thou not see how the nurse in the earliest days of its childhood sometimes ties the little one in its cradle, and at times is ever laying it on her bosom; sometimes strikes it hard and sometimes soothes it; sometimes puts it away from her and repels it, sometimes kindly kisses its cheek and again caresses it and bears its grief? A stranger is angry with the nurse when he sees this, and sighs; he says to it, The nurse is not kind, the child is of little account with her. How shouldst thou know that the nurse is right? Such is always the condition of her work.

God too, according to his compact, performs his whole duty towards his slave; He gives the daily food that is required, sometimes disappointment, sometimes victory; sometimes He sets a jewelled crown upon his head, sometimes He leaves him needy with only a copper.

Be thou contented with God's ordinance; or if not, then cry aloud and complain before the Qâzî, that he may release thee from His decree! A fool is he who thinks thus! Whatever it is,--whether misfortune or prosperity,--it is an unmixed blessing, and the evil only transitory. He who brings the world into being with '*Be, and it was*,'--how, how shall He do evil to the creatures of the world? Good and evil exist not in the world of the Word; the names 'good' and 'evil' belong to thee and to me. When God created the regions of the earth He created no absolute evil; death is destruction for this one, but wealth for that; poison is food to this, and death to that.

If the face of the mirror were black like its back, no one would look at it; the usefulness belongs to the face of the mirror, even though its back be stuffed with jewels. The bright-faced sun is good, be its back black or white; if the peacock's foot were like its feathers, it would shine splendid both by night, and day.

## IN PRAISE OF HIS OMNIPOTENCE.

He is the Pourtrayer of the outward forms of our earthly bodies; He is the Discerner of the images of our inmost hearts. He is the Creator of existent and non-existent, the Maker of the hand and what it holds. He made a wheel of pure emerald, and on the wheel he bound silver jars; He caused a candle and candlestick to revolve in the heavens in the path of the ignoble. Before His creation was non-existence; eternal being belongs to His Essence alone. He made Intelligence proclaimer of His power; He made matter capable of receiving form. To Intelligence He gave the path of vigilance; what thinkest thou of Intelligence?

How can the artist of the pen picture forth in man the image of the Eternal? Fire and wind and water and earth and sky, and Reason and Spirit above the sky, and the angels in the middle place, wisdom and life and abstract form,-- know, that all come into being by command, and the command is God's.

He is the origin and root of material things, the Creator of beneficence, and thanks, and the thankful man. In the high-road from this life to the next He has associated action and power with this world of generation and corruption. In the world of the Word His Omnipotence made power pregnant with action, made its place for whatever comes into action, created its product for whatever possesses power.

## ON THE PROVERBS AND ADMONITIONS 'POVERTY IS BLACKNESS OF THE FACE' (THE RECITAL OF PROVERBS IS THE BEST OF DISCOURSES) AND 'THE WORLD IS A HOUSE OF DEPARTURE AND CHANGING AFFAIRS AND MIGRATION.'

Keep thy blackness, thou canst not do without it; for blackness admits no change of colour. With blackness of face there goes happiness; a blushing face seldom causes joy. The scorched pursuer is black of face before the flame of his heart's desire; though in tribulation, the ugly Ethiopian finds gladness in his blackness of face; his gladness comes not from his beauty, his happiness comes from his sweet odour. Brighter than the splendour of the new moon is the display of the moon of Bilâl's shoe; if thou dost not wish thy heart's secret known, keep thy blackness of face in both worlds, since for him who seeks his desire, day tears the veil and night spreads it.

Withhold thy hand from these vain lusts; know, desire is poison, and the belly as a snake; the serpent of desire, if it bite thee, will soon despatch thee from the world. For in this path in evil there is good; the water of life is in the midst of darkness. What sorrow has the heart from blackness? For night is pregnant with day, and the men who are now imprisoned without food or drink in this old ruin throw aside all instruction when they march proudly in the garden of God.

Everything except God, all that is of earth, is aside from the path of the true faith. Loss of self is the hidden goal of all; the refuge of the pure soul is with the Word. O thou, who hast rolled up the carpet of time, who hast passed beyond the four and the nine, pass at one step beyond life and reason, that so thou mayst arrive at God's command. Thou canst not see, forasmuch as thou art blind at night; and in the day too hast but one eye, like the wisdom of fools. I do not speak to thee with wink and nod, but in God's way, with mystical significations and allegories.

Till thou pass beyond the false, God is not there; the perfect truth belongs not to this half-display. Know, that as provision for the journey to the eternal world, *lâ khair* is your strength and *lâ shai* your gold; *lâ khair* is the strength of the rich, as *lâ shai* is the wisdom of the wine-drinkers.

## ON THE NEED OF GOD, AND INDEPENDENCE OF ALL BESIDE HIM.

He is wholly independent of me and thee in his plans; what matters infidelity or faith to His Independence? What matters that or this to His Perfection '? Know that God exists in real existence; in pursuance of His decree and just designs, the Independent seeks thy favours, the Guardian gives thee thanks. The wolf and Yûsuf appear to thee to be small and great; but with Him, Yûsuf and wolf are the same. What, to His Mercy, matters opposition or help? What, to His Wrath, are Moses and Pharaoh?

Thy service or thy rebellion are an honour or a shame to thee, but with Him the colour of both is the same. What honour has He from Reason, or from the lightning, what greatness from the soul, or the sky? The soul and the heavens are His creatures. Happy the man who is chosen of Him.

The heavens and He who causes them to revolve are as the millstone and the miller; the supreme Disposer and the obedient Reason are as the carver's self and the matter he shapes. The motion of the restless heavens and of the earth is as it were an ant in the mouth of a dragon; the dragon does not swallow the ant, and the revolution of the unconscious heavens sweeps on. He has imposed its task upon the mill-wheel of misfortune, itself unmindful and closed round by annihilation. Think of thy life as an atom in His time. His banquet as accompanied by His affliction. Thou knowest that thy goblet has four feet for movement; yet though thou be persevering in His service thou wilt not reach His path but by His grace. When will the slave who wishes to attain to God reach Him by means of reason, or by hand and foot? When will he attain to God, who in his own body attains (only to the recognition of) his hands and feet?

## ON SELF-ABASEMENT AND HUMILITY.

Lowliness befits thee, violence suits thee not; a, naked man frantic in a bee-house is out of place. Leave aside thy strength, betake thyself to lowliness, that so thou mayest trample the heights of heaven beneath thy feet; for God knows that, rightly seen, thy strength is a lie, and thy lowliness truth. If thou layest claim to strength and wealth, thou hast a blind eye and a deaf ear. Thy face and thy gold are red, thy coat is of many colours,--then look to find thy honour disgrace, thy peace strife. Come not to God's door in the dust of thy strength, for in this road it is through lowliness that thou becomest a hero. This comes not of discharging thy debt, but from bartering thy indigence. Look not on His Omnipotence with thy impotent eye O my master, commit not such an outrage.

So long as thou art thy own support, clothe thyself, and eat; but if thou art upheld by Him, thou shalt neither sew nor tear. All that exists, O friend, exists through Him; thine own existence is as a pretence,--speak not folly. If thou lose thyself, thy dust becomes a mosque; if thou hold to thyself, a fire-temple: if thou hold to thyself, thy heart is hell; if thou lose thyself, heaven. If thou lose thyself, all things are accomplished, thy selffulness is an untrained colt. Thou art thou,--hence spring love and hate; thou art thou,--hence spring infidelity and faith. Remain a slave, without lot or portion; for an angel is neither hungry nor full. Fear and hope have driven away fortune from thee; when thy self has gone, hope and fear are no more.

The owl that frequents the palace of the king is a bird of ill-omen, ill-fated and guilty, when it is contented in its solitude, its feathers are finer than the splendour of the phœnix. Musk is spoilt by water and by fire; but to the musk-bladder what matters wet or dry? What matters, at His door, a Muslim or a fire-worshipper? What, before him, a fire-temple or a monk's cell? Fire-worshipper and Christian, virtuous and guilty, all are seekers, and He the sought.

God's essence is independent of cause; why seekest thou now a place for cause? The sun of religion comes not forth by instruction; the moon goes down when the light of the truth shines out. If the holy man is good, it is well for him; if the king is bad, what is that to us? To be saved, do thou thyself persevere in good; why contendest thou with God's decree and predestination? In this halt of but a week, to be is not to be, to come is to go.

Recite the word '*hastening on*'; (Qur. 57:12) for in the resurrection the believer calls "*Make way!*" Mustafâ exclaimed 'How excellent!'; through this the hand of Moses became a moon, the Friend of God grew pitiful; (Qur.

9:116) the *wâw* of *awwah* gave him the sincerity of his faith, the majesty and beauty of his belief,--then when the *wâw* goes out of *awwah* there remains but *âh*, a sigh,--how wonderful! *Âh* remains, a memorial of Him; His religion remains as a manifestation of Him.

Before the trumpet sounds kill thou thyself with the sword of indigence; if they accept it, thou art at rest; if not, think of what has happened as if it had not been. If thou come small or great to the door of the Absolute, or if thou come not at all, what is that to Him? Shall the day subsist for the sake of the cock? it will appear at its own time. What is thy existence, what thy non-existence to Him? Many like thee come to His door.

When the fountain of light starts forth, it has no need of any to scourge it on; yet all this magnificence is but water and earth,--the pure life and soul are there. What can the '*Make way!*' of a handful of straw effect? His own light alone cries '*Make way!*' That lamp of thine is thy trust in thyself; the sun comes forth of himself in brightness, and this flame the cold wind cannot extinguish, while half a sneeze wrests from that its life.

So then your road lies not in this street; if there be a road, it is the road of your sighs. You are all far from the road of devotion, you are like asses straying for months and years deluded with vain hopes. Since thou art sometimes virtuous, sometimes wicked, thou fearest for thyself, hast hope in thyself; but when thy face of wisdom and of shame grows white,--go, know thou that fear and hope are one.

*

## ON THE JUSTICE OF THE PRINCE AND THE SECURITY OF HIS SUBJECTS.

`Umar one day saw a group of boys on a certain road all engaged in play and everyone boasting of himself; everyone was in haste to wrestle, having duly bared his head in Arab fashion. When `Umar looked towards the boys, fear of him tore the curtain of their gladness; they all fled from him in haste, except `Abdu'l-lâh b. Zubair. `Umar said to him, "Why didst thou not fly from before me?" He said, "Why should I fly from before thee, O beneficent one? Thou art not a tyrant, nor I guilty."

If a prince is pious and just, his people, are glad in his justice but if his inclination is towards tyranny, he plunges his country in ruin. When thou hast provisioned thyself with justice, thy steed has passed beyond both halting-places. What matters acceptance or rejection, good or evil, to him who knows his own virtue? Be virtuous,--thou wilt escape an aching head; if thou be bad, thou breakest the whole compact. So stand in wonder at His justice that thou losest memory of all else but of Him.

## ON CELEBRATING THE PRAISE OF GOD.

To call on the name of friends, and the unhappy ones of this world, how thinkest thou of it? It is like calling on old women. Oppression, if He ordain it, is all justice; a life without thought of Him is all wind. He laughs who is brought to tears through Him; but that heart is an anvil that thinks not on Him. Thou art secure when thou pronouncest His name,--thou keepest a firm footing on thy path; make thou thy tongue moist, like earth, with remembrance of Him, that He may fill thy mouth, like the rose, with gold. He fills with life the soul of the wise man; the heart of the lover of self He leaves thirsty. That thy purpose and judgment may be true, have not His door at all; to pay heed to those about us is the act of a thoughtless fool.

## CONCERNING THE PIOUS DISCIPLE AND THE GREAT MASTER.

Thaurî, by way of obsequiousness and in anxiety to acquire a good reputation, asked an excellent question of Bâyazîd Bistâmi; weeping, he said, "O Master, tell me, who is unjust?" His master, giving him a draught out of the law, answered him and said, "Unjust is that ill-fated one who for one! moment of the day and night in negligence forgets Him: he is nest His submissive slave." If thou forget Him for one breath, there is none so shamelessly unjust as thou; but if thou be present and commemorate His name, thy being is lost in the fulfilment of His commands. So think upon Him that in thy heart and soul. thou lapse not into forgetfulness even for an instant. Keep in mind this saying of that ever-watchful traveller on this road, the impetuous lion. '*And worship thou the Lord in prayer as if thou sawest Him;*' and if thou do not thus, thou wilt be forced to cry '*Help, help!*' So worship Him in both worlds, as if thou sawest Him with thine outward eye; though thine eye sees Him not, thy Creator sees thee.

The commemoration of God exists only in the path of conflict it exists not in the assembly of the contemplation: though remembrance of Him be thy guide at first, in the end remembrance is naught.

Inasmuch as the diver seeks pearls in the seas, it is the water too that kills his cry; in absence the dove calls 'where?'--if present, why recite 'He'? Those in His presence are rich in His majesty; weep thou, if absence is thy portion.

Listen to the ringdove's plaint of yearning,--two grains of barley changes it into joy; but he who seeks the only true contentment, seeks the light of the Unity in the grave. To him the tomb is the garden of Paradise; heaven is unlovely in his eyes. Then wilt thou be present, when in the abode of peace thou art present in soul, not in body; whilst thou art in this land of fruitless search, thou art either all back or all front; but when the soul of the seeker has gone forward a few paces out of this land, love seizes the bridle. Unbelief is death, religion life,-- this is the pith of all that men have said.

Whoso for one moment takes delight in himself, he is imprisoned in hell and anguish for years. Who then shall have this honour and high dignity conferred upon him? Only he who possesses the principle of Islâm; in loving, and in striving towards that world, one must not talk about one's life; those who travel on this road know nothing of grief for life and sorrow of soul. When thou hast passed out of this world of fruitless search, then seek thou in that the fountain of life.

# CONCERNING THE HOUSE OF DECEPTION.

Death comes as the key of the house of the Secret; without death the door of true religion opens not. While this world stays, that is not; while thou existest, God is not thine. Know, thy soul is a sealed casket; the love-pearl within is the light of thy faith. The Past sealed the writing, and delivered it for thee to the Future; as long as thou shalt depend for thy life upon the revolutions of Time, thou shalt not know what is inside. Only the hand of death shall unloose the binding of the book, of God the Exalted, the Glorious. So long as the breath of man flies not from thee, the morning of thy true faith will not dawn in thy soul's East.

Thou wilt not reach the door or the King's pavilion without experiencing the heat and cold of the world: at present thou knowest naught of the invisible world, canst not distinguish faults from virtues; the things of that world are not those of sense, are not like the other things of wont. The soul reaches His presence, and is at rest; and what is crooked then is seen to be straight.

When thou arrivest in the presence of the decree the soul sets forth, and like a bird leaves its cage for the garden; the horse of religion becomes familiar with the verdant meadow. Whilst thou livest true religion appears not; the night of thy death brings forth its day. On this subject a man of wisdom, whose words are as a mufti's decision, said, "Through desire and transgression men have gone to sleep; when death shows his face, they awake." All the people of this world are asleep, all are living in a vicious world the desire that goes beyond this is use and custom, and not religion for the religion which is only of this life is not religion, but empty trifling.

To knock at the door of non-existence is religion and fortune knocking little comes of being little. He who esteems of small account the substance of this world, say to him, "Look thou on Mustafâ and Adam"; and he who seeks for increase, say to him, "Look thou on `Âd and on Qârûn; the foot of the one clave to his stirrup, the other lived pierced through with terror; the Eternal destroyed the foot of the one; remorse turned the hand of the other into a reed; the dire blast falls on `Âd, the dust of execration is the abode of Qârûn.

What harm is it, if from fear of misfortune thou sacrifice thyself like wild rue for the sake of virtue? Inflame not thy cheek before the men of the Path; burn thyself, like wild rue; thou hast the wisdom and religion of a fool if thou pretendest to eminence before God. Let not man weave a net about himself; rather the lion will break his cage. O thou, who art sated with thyself,--that is hunger; and thou, who bendest double in penitence,--that is prayer. When thou art freed from thine own body and soul, then thou findest isolation and eminence. Display not at all thy city-inflaming countenance; when thou hast done so, go, burn wild rue. What is that beauty of thine? it is thy lust; and what is thy wild rue? it is thine own being. When thy lip touches the threshold of true religion, Jesus, son of Mary, becomes thy sleeve. In this quest do thou melt thyself; adventure thy life and soul in the path of fidelity; strive thou, that so through non-existence thou mayest pass to existence; that thou mayest be drunk with the wine of God. The ball and stick of the universe are in the hand of him whom true religion makes to live; when thy soul becomes drunk with this draught, thou hast reached the summit; from being naught thou comest into existence.

Every freed man of that place is a slave, bound by the foot, with a ring in his ear; but those bonds are better than the steed of fortune; but that ring is better than the striped garments of Arabia and a throne. The bonds that He imposes, account a crown; and if He gives thee sackcloth, reckon it brocade; for He bestows benefits, and He gives beauty; He is kind, and He is bounteous.

Seeing that thou art needy, what dost thou with Gladness, and what with Cleverness, both bought with a price? Be glad in Him, and clever in His religion, that thou mayest find acceptance and honour with Him. That man is wise whom He lifts up; joyful is he whom He abandons not; and fortunate, who is His slave, approved by Him in all his works. When thou hast cast these branches, and hast grappled with death, thou wilt no longer turn away from death, and shalt come to know the world of Life. When thy hand reaches the branch of death, thy foot treads the palace of power; the foot which is far from the dome of right guidance is not a foot.--it is a drunken brain.

## ON GIVING THANKS.

Ingratitude's only seat is the door of sorrow; thankfulness arrives with certainty at the treasure. (Qur. 14:7) Utter thy thanks for the sake of increase, of the hidden world, and of the sight of God; then when thou hast become patient of His decree He will name thee 'giver of thanks'; whoso presses forwards towards God, speaks not without uttering his thanks to God. Who can tell the sweetness of giving thanks to Him? Who can pierce the pearl of the celebration of His name? He bestows, and He gives the reward; He speaks, and He imparts the answer. Whatsoever He took away from thee of kindness or show of love, the same or more than that He gives back to thee. (Qur. 2:100) If every hair became a tongue, and each an interpreter at thanksgiving's door to swell thereby His thanks, they could not utter due thanks for the divine grace of the power to give thanks.

Then let men seek to give thanks for His mercies; if they utter them, it is even through Him they do so,--body and soul drunk with His decree, the heart singing "*O Lord, thanks!*" And if not, then as far as regards the path of knowledge and prudence, woman and man, young and old, are blind of eye in the world of lust, are naked of body like ants and flies.

## ON HIS WRATH AND HIS KINDNESS.

The pious are those who give thanks for His kindness and mercy, the unbelievers those who complain of His wrath and jealousy. When God becomes angry, thou seest in the eyes what is rightly in the spring. His wrath and His kindness, appearing in the newly-formed world, are the cause of the error of the Guebre and the doubt of the Magian. His kindness and His wrath are imprinted on the pulpit and the gallows; the rendering of thanks to Him is the mansion of honour, and forgetfulness of Him, of disgrace. His kindness is comfort for men's lives, His wrath a fire for their souls; His kindness rejoices the slave; His wrath makes man its mock. When the *lâm* of His kindness shows itself, the *dâl* of fortune gains the victory; if the *qâf* of His wrath rushes forth, it melts Mount Qâf like silver. The whole world dreads His anger and His subtlety; the virtuous and the ungodly are alike in their terror. When His kindness mixes the draught of exhilaration, the shoe of the *Sûfî* mounts to ecstasy; when His wrath comes forth again, ecstasy draws in its head like a tortoise. His wrath melts even His beloved; His kindness cherishes the beggar. He it is who nourishes thy soul in unbelief or in the faith, He who gives thy soul the power of choice. Thy life's soul lives through His kindness; for by His kindness thy life endures.

By His disposing wrath and kindness He brings to life the dead, to death the living; His wisdom cares for the slave, His favour accomplishes our undertakings. When His wrath came forth in conflict, it killed the country's king by means of an impotent gnat. Then when He saddled the horse of kindness, he caused the food of worms to gather locusts; through God he abode in wisdom and right counsel,--the worms were silver, the locusts gold; and as in the midst of God's favour he suffered a proving trial, when again in favour he laughed at his misfortunes. When His wrath spreads the snare, He turns the form of Bil'âm into a dog; (Qur. 7:174-5) when His kindness worked, He brought the dog of the Companions of the Cave into the cavern. The magicians through His kindness exclaimed "*No harm*"; (Qur. 26:49-50) His wrath caused 'Azâzîl to say, "*I am better.*" (Qur. 38:77)

With God no good and no evil has power; with whom can it be said that there exists no one else in the world? No matter whether small or great, His wrath and His kindness reach everyone alike. Emperors humble themselves on His path, heroes bow down their heads at His door; kings are as dust before His door, Pharaohs fly in terror from before Him. By means of a Turkish demon, a slave just bought, He overthrew a hundred thousand standards of war; while yet he had no more than a couple of retainers, he folded up the carpet of a hungry band.

74

If He says to the dead, Come forth, the dead comes forth, dragging his winding-sheet behind him; and if He says to the living, Die, he dies on the spot, though he be a prince. The people are proud of heart through His kindness because of the respite He gives them they fear not at all; but whoso manifests presumption in His kingdom has broken away from the straight road. His poison shall be the sufficient food of the champions, His wrath an adequate bridle for the haughty; He has broken the necks of heroes by His wrath; to the weak He has given a double share of His kindness. The quickness of His forgiveness obliterates the marks of our pleading from the path of speech; He gives shelter to him who repents of his sin, and cleanses his pages of the crime; His forgiveness outruns the fault,--"*My mercy outstrips*" is a wonderful saying. He is the giver of the soul; not, as we are, a creature to whom a soul is given; He holds up the veil, He does not tear it as we do. He is thy shepherd, and thou choosest the wolf; He invites thee, and thou remainest in want; He is thy guardian, and thou thyself carest not; O well done, thou senseless sinning fool! He reforms our nature within us; kinder than ourselves is He to us; mothers have not for their children such love as He bestows. The worthless He makes worthy by His kindness; from His servants He accepts thankfulness and patience as sufficient. His beneficence has shut the door of sense against the eye of wisdom and uprightness, and opened to it the path of the spirit.

Since His clemency has established thee thou art secure against the plunderers; the mountain-dweller ever escapes in the plain the affliction of the north-east wind. Though invisible to us, He knows our faults; His pardon can wash them away. His knowledge has concealed our imperfection; the secret thou hast not yet spoken, He has heard. The sons of men, ever unjust and ignorant, talk in folly of God's kindness; He works good, and ye work evil: He knows the hidden things, and ye are full of fault. Behold, after thy so many doubts, this care of the Knower of the hidden for a wicked world; had it not been pure favour on His part, how could a handful of earth have come to wear a crown?

The alighting-place of His pardon is on the plain of sin, the army of His kindness comes out to meet our sighs; when the sigh of the knower of God raises the veil, hell seizes its shield from fear of Him. His forgiveness grants itself to our sins; His mercy descends to bestow benefits. Thou hast committed the iniquity, yet He keeps faith with thee; He is more true to thee than thou art to thyself. His bounty brought thee into activity; otherwise how could this market have been set up on earth? Whoso becomes nonexistent, to him is given existence; whoso slips receives a helping hand. He it is who takes the hand of the friendless, and chooses weeds like us. Forasmuch as He is pure, He desires the pure; the Knower of the hidden desires the dust.

## ON HIS, OMNISCIENCE, AND HIS KNOWLEDGE OF THE MINDS OF MEN.

He knows the draught of each of His creatures; He has given it, and He can give its opposite. He is the Creator of thy wisdom; but His wisdom is untainted by the passage of thought. He knows concerning thee what is in thy heart, for He is the Creator both of thy heart and of thy clay. Dost thou think that He knows as thou knowest? then is the ass of thy nature stuck fast in thy clay. He sees what is best for His creatures before the desire is formed; He knows the mind before the secret thought exists. He knows what is in thy heart; before thou speakest He performs the work. God brings joy and takes away sorrow; God knows our secrets, and He keeps them safe.

Silence before Him is the gift of tongues; thy life's food thou receivest from a table bare of bread; man's desire cannot wish for such things as He has prepared for him. He knows the condition of His creatures; He sees it, and can give accordingly; He has prepared for thee thy place in Paradise, that to-morrow thou mayest enter into joy. It is enough that He speaks,--be thou dumb and speak not; it is enough that He seeks, remain thou a cripple, and run not to and fro. In presence of the power and omniscience of God, feebleness and ignorance are best: feebleness makes thee wise, weakness confers eminence on thee. Whoso can make existence non-existent, can also change nonexistence into existence. He in His mercy arrests the rhythmical forces in the wombs for the due constituting and establishing of the offspring; and forasmuch as His inscrutability pourtrayed thy form, knowest thou not that thou canst not remain hidden? He knows thy case better than thyself; why frequentest thou the neighbourhood of folly and deceit? Speak not of thy heart's sorrow, for He is speaking; seek thou not for Him, for He is seeking.

He perceives the touch of an ant's foot, though in night and darkness the ant move on a rock, if a stone moves in the dark night in the depth of the water, His knowledge sees it; if there be a worm in the heart of a rock, whose body is smaller than an atom, God by His knowledge knows its cry of praise, and its hidden secret. To thee He has given guidance in the path; to the worm He has given its sustenance in the rock. No soul has ever rested in patience apart from Him no understanding deceived Him by its subtlety. He is ever aware of the minds of men,--ponder thou this, and thy duty is fulfilled. If thou turn thy face from evil usage, thy mind shall preserve the true religion of Islâm; but since thou choosest to hold false ideas of His clemency, thou shalt have no light, but hell-fire in thy heart; for since thou wilt not take account of His knowledge, O man, cherish no hope of clemency from Him. His omniscience kindles the lamp of the understanding; but His clemency teaches nature to sin; were not His clemency a perpetual refuge, how could a servant dare to sin?

If then thou committest a sin, that sin falls under one of two cases; if thou thinkest that God knows not, I say to thee, Well done, O thorough-going infidel! and if thou thinkest that God knows, and still thou committest it,-- Bravo, impudent one, and vile! Myself I acknowledge that no man knows thy secrets; God knows,--God is not less than man; and I take it that if He hides this forgiveness from thee, is it not that His omniscience knows that it is thus with thee? Then turn from this vile conduct of thine; otherwise on the day of thy resurrection thou wilt forthwith see thyself drowning in the sea of thy shame.

## CONCERNING HIS BENEFICENCE,--AND VERILY HE IS THE PROVIDER OF PROVISIONS.

When He lays the table of its food before the creature, He provides a fare more ample than the eater's needs; life and days and daily food come to all from Him; happiness and fortune are from Him. He supplies the daily bread of each, nor seals the door of the storehouse; infidel and true believer, wretched and prosperous, to all their daily food and life renewed. While the _Há_ of necessity is still in their throat, the _Jím_ of His munificence has given His creatures their sustenance. Except by bread we cannot live, and appetite is our only relish; He shuns not His servants when they turn to Him,--He has given the relish, He will give the bread too.

Thy bread and life are in the treasury of God; thou dost not hold, according to His word, that it is He. If thy daily bread be in China, thy horse of acquisition is ready saddled to bear thee speedily to it, or to bring it to thee whilst thou art sleeping. Has He not said to thee, I am thy Sustainer, the Knower of what is hidden and the Knower of what is manifest; I gave life, I give the means of livelihood; whatsoever thou askest, I give forthwith? Know that, like the day, the matter of thy daily bread is well assured, for thy daily bread is a present which the day brings with it; forasmuch as the kindness of God is on thee, thou boldest thy life as a pledge for thy food. Take thought for thy life, and thou hast done the same for thy bread; loaf succeeds loaf as far as the edge of the grave. Hold firmly to this pledge, and eat thy bread; and when the pledge passes from thee, still shalt thou eat the food of Life. Life without bread God gave to none, for life endures through bread; and when life quits the body, know for a certainty that now indeed sustenance has reached thee.

The ignoble fear for their daily bread; the generous man does not eat his food warmed up a second time. The lion eats not his prey alone; when he is satisfied, he abandons the rest. It is for women to hoard up the old; to men new sustenance with the new day. Thy daily bread is a charge on the All-knowing and All-powerful,--be not angry against prince or minister; it comes from God's door, and not by teeth or throat or pipe.

The lordship of a house is a lordship with sorrow, especially for him who has no wealth or treasure; the lordship of a house is all sorrow and desire,--leave aside the *house*, and *God* is sufficient for thee. Let thy trust at all times be on God, rather than on mill and sack; for if the clouds give thee no water for a year, I foresee that thy affairs will be altogether ruined.

## A STORY.

An old man put forth his head, and seeing his field dried up I spoke thus:--"O Lord of both new and old, our food is in Thy hands, do what thou wilt. The sustenance Thou givest to fair and foul depends not on tears of cloud nor smiles of field; I well know Thou art the Uncaused Sustainer; my life and my food, all comes from Thee. Thy one is better than thousands of thousands, for Thy little is not a little." A flame from Him, and a hundred thousand stars appear; a drop from Him, and a hundred thousand palm-trees spring up. He who is in fear about his daily food is not a man,--truly he is less than a woman.

## A STORY.

Hast thou not heard how in a rainless time some birds received their food from a Magian's door? Many Muslims spoke to him, and among them one clever and eloquent--"Though the little birds take your corn, yet this generosity of yours will not find acceptance." Said the Magian, "If He does not choose me, still He sees my toil; since He himself is kind and generous, He does not think the same of niggardliness as of liberality."

Ja`far sacrificed his arm in His Path; instead of arms God gave him wings. None shall discover thy work but God; truly nothing can happen to thee from men. Pay no heed to the doing and bustling of men, fasten thy mind on Him, and thou hast escaped from sorrow and bondage. So far as thou canst, take thou no friend but Him; take men not into thy account at all. Your bread is laid up in God's eternity; His friendship He gives you,--it is your life; know that both of these are represented in the world of love and search by the Persian *water* and the Arabic *father.*

## ON THE DESIRE FOR GOD.

So long as thou art a stranger to the light of Moses, thou art blind to the day, like the bird of Jesus; since thou hast no knowledge of the path of poverty, thou art in hiding, like the inside of an onion. First, for the sake of His comforting love, do thou make thy head thy foot, like the reed, and continue seeking Him; that by thy perfect search thou mayest reach that place, where thou knowest thou needest seek no more.

Did not an indolent one, when he heard murmurs of sloth on his heart's tongue, ask `Alî, "Say, O Prince, illuminer of the soul, is the dark night better, or the day?" Murtazâ said, "Hear, O questioner; yield not to this backsliding; for to the lovers in this soul-inflaming path the fire of the secret is better than the splendour of the day." He whose soul the path has fired stays not behind on foot at the halting-place; in that world where love tells the secret, thou no longer art, thy reason no longer endures.

## ON AFFECTION AND ISOLATION.

The lovers are drunk in His Presence, their reason in their sleeve and their soul in their hand. Lo, when they urge the Burâq of their heart on towards Him, they cast all away under his feet; they throw down life and heart in His path. and make themselves of His company. In the face of his belief in the Unity, there exists for him no old or new; all is naught, naught; He alone is. What worth have reason and life in his eyes? the heart and the true faith pursue the road together. The veil of the lovers is very transparent; the tracings on these veils are very delicate. Love's conqueror is he who is conquered by love; '*love*' inverted will itself explain this to thee. When the clouds fall away from the Sun, the world of love is filled with light. The cloud is dark and murky as a Magian, but water may be useful as well as harmful;--a little of it is man's life, but his life is destroyed by too much of it; so he who believes in the Unity is the beloved of His Presence, though affection, too, is a veil over His glory.

He is not in evil plight to whom He addresses His instruction. What then is evil?--to be the friend who toils. Look at the letters of *mahabbat* (friendship); the very word *mihnat* (labour) is shown in its characters. O thou who lovest the Beauty of the Presence of the Invisible, till thou seek for the meeting with His face thou wilt never drink the draught of communion with Him, nor taste the sweetness of inward converse with Him. Since thou knowest the One, and assertest the One, why search after the two, and three, and four? Together with *alif* go *be* and *te*,--count *be* and *te* an idol, and *alif* God.

Continue to ply hand and foot in search; when thou reachest the sea, talk not of the rill. Since glory and shame have made of thee a slave, O youth, what hast thou to do with the Eternal? Thou art but newly come into existence,--talk not of the Eternal, thou who dost not know thy head from thy foot. There are a hundred thousand obstructions in thy path; thy courage fails, and falls short; thy talk is trickery still, still thou remainest in the snare. Betake thyself at once to the ocean of righteousness and true religion, thy body naked like wheat-grains, or like Adam; that so He may approve thy complete renunciation; then see that thou meddle not again with these useless encumbrances. Thou art as yet a follower of Satan; how canst thou become a man without repenting?

When He admits thee in His court, ask from Him no object of desire,--ask Himself; when thy Lord has chosen thee for friendship, thy unabashed eye has seen all there is to see. The world of love suffers not duality,--what talk is this of Me and Thee?

When thy Thee-ness leaves thee, fortune will uplift thy state and seat; in a compact of intimacy it is not well to claim to be a friend, and then-still *Me* and *Thee*! How shall he that is free become a slave? How canst thou fill a vessel already full? Go thou, all of thee, to His door; for whoso in the world shall present himself there in part only, is wholly naught. When thou hast reached to the kiss and love-glance of the Friend, count poison honey from Him, and the thorn a flower.

For the rust on the mirror of the free, *No* is the nail-parer,---with it cut off existence. Be not filled with thy incapacity time after time, as a boat is filled; dost thou not read in God's book that those who die are not dead but living? (Qur. 3:164)

Receive alike good and evil, fair and foul; whatever God sends thee, take it to thy soul. Did not ʿAzâzîl, receiving from God both His mercy and His curse, deem them both alike? Whatsoever he obtained from God, good or evil, he held both equal. But the likeness of him who waits at the door of princes is as a sail in unskilled hands.

## ON RENUNCIATION AND STRENUOUS ENDEAVOUR.

Whoso desires to be lord of his isolation and whoso seeks to guard his seclusion, must take no ease within, nor adorn himself without; that praise which is bestowed on outward seeming imports the abandonment of true praise and adornment. The beggar asks bread at the door of the king; so the lover begs food for his soul. On the path, naked and fearless, he has cast water and fire and earth to the winds. Standing on the plain of the signposts of time, what matter fools to him, what the philosopher of the age? O brother, hold thy liver as roast meat in the fire of renunciation, not a broth. The mean-spirited dog seeks a bone; the lion's whelp seeks the marrow of life. The lovers have sacrificed soul and heart, and day and night have made His memory their food.

The man of high resolves seeks not bondage; a dog is a dog, made happy by a bite.

If revelation become a restraint on thee, make of it a shoe and beat thy head with it; talk fewer superfluities, and keep thy weakness before thee; leave the bone to the dogs. In virtue of thy essential nature thou hast obtained a high station; then why be mean in spirit like a dog? On the man of high endeavour both worlds are bestowed; but whoso is mean-spirited like a dog, like a dog runs about after a meal.

If thou desirest to possess thy soul free from the body, *Lâ* is as a gallows,--keep company with it. How can pure Divinity admit thee till thy humanity has been uplifted on the gallows?--for on the path to divinity thy souls will suffer many crucifixions. Put an end to all imitation and speculation, that thy heart may become the house of God. As long as thy existence is with thee in thy soul, the ka`ba is a tavern, though thou serve Him; but if thy soul has parted from thy existence, through thee an idol temple becomes the Inhabited House.

O seeker of taverns, full of wretchedness, thou art but an ass's son, and asses are thy fathers! Thy understanding is muddied with thy Self and thy Existence; thy reason's sight is dark before that other world. Thine own soul it is that distinguishes unbelief and true religion; of necessity it colours thy vision. Selflessness is happy, selfulness most unhappy; cast away the cat from under thy arm. In the Eternal, unbeliefs and religions are not; such things exist not if the nature be pure.

## ON FOLLOWING THE PATH OF THE HEREAFTER.

All this knowledge is but a trifling matter; the knowledge of the journey on God's road is otherwise, and belongs to the man of acuter vision. What, for the man of wisdom and true religion, whose bread and speech are alike of wheat, distinguishes that path and points it out? Inquire its mark from the Speaker and the Friend.

And if, O brother, thou also ask of me, I answer plainly and with no uncertainty, 'To turn thy face towards the world of life, to set thy foot upon outward prosperity, to put out of mind rank and reputation, to bend one's back double in His service, to purify ourselves from evil, to strengthen the soul in wisdom.'

What is the provision for such a journey, O heedless one? By looking on the Truth to cut oneself off from the false; to leave the abode of those who strive with words, and to sit before the silent; to journey from the works of God to His attributes, and from His attributes to the mansion of the knowledge of Him; then from knowledge to the world of the secret, then to reach the threshold of poverty; then when thou art become the friend of poverty, thy Soul destroys thy impure Self; I thy Self becomes Soul inside thee; it becomes ashamed of all its doings, and casting aside all its possessions is melted on its path of trial; then when thy Self has been melted in thy body, thy Soul has step by step accomplished its work; then God takes away its, poverty from it,--when poverty is no more, God remains.

Not in folly nor ignorance spoke Bâyazîd, if he said '*Glory to me;*' so too the tongue that spoke the supreme secret moved truly when it said, '*I am God.*' When he proclaimed to the back the secret he had learned from the face, it became his executioner and killed him; his secret's day-time became as night, but God's word was what he spoke; when in the midst of the rabble he suddenly disclosed, unauthorized, the secret, his outward form was given to tile gallows, his inward being was taken by the Friend; when his life's soul could speak no longer, his heart's blood divulged the secret.

He spoke well who said in his ecstacy, *Leave thyself, O son, and come hither.* From thee to the Friend is not long; thyself art the road, then set thy feet on it, that with the eye of Godhead thou mayest see the handwriting of the Lord of power and the land of spirits.

When shall we be separated from our Selves,--*I* and *thou* departed and God remaining? the heart arrived at God's threshold, the Soul, saying, Here am I, enter thou. When by the doorway of renunciation heart and soul have reached the dome of a true belief in the Unity, the soul locks itself in the embrace of the Houris, the heart walks proudly in the sight of the Friend.

O thou who knowest not the life that comes of the juice of the grape, how long then wilt thou be drunk with the grape's outward form? Why boastest thou falsely that thou art drunk? So that they say, 'The fellow has drunk butter-milk!' If thou drink wine, say naught; the drinker of butter-milk too will guard his secret. Why seekest thou? Deem it not like thy soul; drink it as thou dost thy faith. Thou knowest not what *mâs* is in Persian; when thou hast eaten it, thou recognizest the taste. When in this ruined hall thou drinkest a cup of wine, I counsel thee put not thy foot outside the house of thy drunkenness, lay down thy head where thou hast drunk the wine; till thou hast drunk it, hold it an unlawful thing, and when thou hast drunk it, rub a clod of earth on thy lips. When with a hundred pains thou hast twice drunk the dregs, I will say, Look at the man's courage! More numerous than asses without head-stalls are all the carrion-hearted wine-drinkers; wine has eaten up and the grape has carried off both their understanding and their soul. In this company of youths, in their cowardice no longer men, if thou speak not, thou remainest true; but if thou speak, thou blasphemest.

How canst thou go forward? there is no place for thee, and how then wilt thou leap? thou hast no foot; he feeds on sorrow for whom there is no place, and he is destitute who has no foot. Those who, freed from being, stand at the door of the true Existence, did not today for the first time gird up their loins at His door; from Eternity the sons of the serving-men, giving up wealth and power, have stood before Love as numerous as ants.

Strive that when death shall come with speed he may find thy soul already in his street. Leave this house of vagabonds: if thou art at His door, remain there; if not, repair thither: for those who are His servants are contented in His Godhead, (Qur. 39:36) ever, their loins of servitude girt up, the lord of the seven heavens even as a slave.

## OF THE LEARNED MAN AND THE FOOL.

The shaikh of Jurjân said to his son, "Thou must have a house in this street for thy private pursuits; and it will be well if the lock be a cunning one." Contrive thy finery in the path of renunciation with its head of the Law, and its secret parts of the Unity; and enter this lodging of trouble and distress like a traveller, and quickly pass on from it. At the door of the garden of *Except God* strip off and make away with thy coat and cap; become naught, that He himself, engaging thee to answer, may with justice call to thee, "*To whom belongs the kingdom?*"

## A STORY.

The saint *Shiblî* said in private converse, after a period of inward communion with God, If, for that I am not far from Him, He give me leave to speak, and with just purpose ask, *To whom belongs the kingdom?* then in sincerity I will answer Him and say, To-day the kingdom belongs to him who from yesterday and the day before has administered it; to-day and to-morrow Thy kingdom, O Mighty over us, is for him whose yesterday and the day before it was. The sword of Thy wrath cuts off the head of the valiant, and then gives back to the head its life.

Know that traffic is good for gain, and the lance of the sun healthful for the sunflower.

When I thou shalt be offended with all but God, Gabriel will appear to thee as naught. No one knows how long the way may be from the word Not to God for while thou holdest to thy Self thou wilt wander day and night, right and left, for thousands of years; then when after laying long toil upon thyself at last thou openest thine eyes, thou seest Self, because of its essential nature and its limitation to conjecture, wandering round about itself, like the ox in a mill. But if, freed from thyself, thou begin at all to labour, thou wilt find admission at this door within two minutes; the two hands of the understanding, holding but *this* distance, are empty; but what *that* distance is, God knows.

O Sikandar, on this path of troubles and in this darkness, do thou, like the prophet Khizr, bring under foot thy jewel of the mine, that so thou mayest obtain the water of life. God will not be thine whilst thou retainest soul and life; both can not be thine,--this and that. Bruise thy Self through months and years, then deem it dead and leave it where it lies; when thou hast finished with thy vile Self, thou hast reached eternal life and joy and Paradise.

Remain unmoved by hope and fear; why contendest thou with Mâlîk and Rizwân? To non-existence, mosque and fire-temple are one; to a shadow, hell and heaven are the same; for him whose guide Love is, infidelity and faith are equally a veil before His door; his own being is the veil before the friend's eyes, hiding the court of God's essence.

## ON TRUST IN GOD.

Set not thy foot in His court with hypocrisy. The men of the Path walk in
trust; if thou hast a constant trust in Him, why not also in His feeding thee?
Bring then thy belongings to the street of trust in God; then fortune will come
out to meet thee. Listen to a story concerning trust. in God, so that thou
remain not a pledge in the hand of the devil; and learn the law of the Path
from a woman besides whom a braggart man shows but contemptibly.

## ON THE TRUST IN GOD SHOWN BY OLD WOMEN.

When Ḥâtim set out for the sanctuary,--he whom thou callest Aṣamm,--when he set out for the Ḥijâz and the Sacred House, making towards the tomb of the Prophet (*on whom be peace!*), there remained behind a colt of his household, with no supplies whatever and owning nothing; he left his wife alone in the house, with no means of support, and set forth on the road; alone and in trouble he left her, her life or death the same to him. Her womanhood was a fellow-traveller with him towards trust in God, for she knew her Provider; she had a friend behind the curtain, being a sharer in God's secret.

The men of the quarter assembled, and all went cheerily to the woman; when they saw her alone and in trouble, they all began at once to ask her her affairs, and by way of advice and counsel, in sympathy said, "When thy husband set out for `Arafât did he leave thee any means of support?" She said, "He did; I am quite contented,--my maintenance is what it was before." Again they said, "How much is thy maintenance? for thy heart is contented and happy." She said, "However long my life lasts, He has given into my hands all the support I need." The other said, "Thou knowest not aught thyself, and what does he know, about thy life?"

She said, "The Giver of my daily bread knows; while life lasts, He will not take away my sustenance." They answered, "He does not give it apart from means; He never gives dates from the willow-tree; thou hast no sort of earthly possessions, and He will not send thee a wallet from heaven." She said, O ye of clouded minds! How long will ye utter folly and perversity? He needs to use a wallet who owns no piece of land; but His are heaven and earth entirely; what He wills He does; His is the authority. He brings it to pass as He desires; sometimes He gives increase, sometimes He takes away."

How long wilt thou talk of trust in God? Thou hearest the name of a man, but art less than a woman. Since on thy journey thou comportest thyself not as men do, go learn how to journey from the women. Thou hast chosen sloth, O body of woman! Alas for the man who is less than a woman!

Look to thy soul, and abandon thy lower nature, for this is as a hawk, and that a heron; that in that place, where it conies to comprehend '*We*' and '*Thou*', when it has been wholly burnt, '*He*' and '*He*' shall remain. Reason, that, living in this world, cannot like soul attain to aught, arrives but as far as itself and reaches not to Him.

The ears of the head are two, the ear of love one; this is for religion, those for doubt; though the ear of the head listens to innumerable things, the ear of love listens only to the story of the One. Those two ears are set on each side of thy head like waterspouts, why dost thou still cry and howl? Thou art but a child;-- go, turn thine eyes away from the devil, lest he put ears on the sides of thy head.

## ON THE KALIMA.

As the inhabited world is computed at twenty-four thousand leagues, so, if thou add the hours of night to those of day, there are twenty-four of those torturers of mankind also. Exchange them, if thou art dexterous and versed in transformations, for the twenty-four letters; the *qâf* of the affirmation of the two testimonies, if these be uttered without deceit or hypocrisy or disputation or contention, will take thee completely out of thy world, bringing thee, not to any instrument, but to *kâf* and *nûn* on this road and in this street, beyond where wisdom is, this is thy sufficient task, to repeat, '*None is God but He.*'

The confession of the faith when reckoned up gives twenty-four as the number of its letters, half of them twelve jewel-caskets from the ocean of life, the other half the twelve zodiacal constellations of the heavens of the faith; the caskets are full of the pearls of hope, the zodiac filled by the moon and sun:--not the pearls of any sea of this world, not the moon and sun of these heavens; but the pearls of the ocean of the world of Power, the moon and sun of the heaven of peace.

# ON THE INTERPRETATION OF THE DREAM.

In the phantoms of sleep He has ordained for men of understanding both fear and hope. When a man has laid down his head in sleep, his tent-ropes are severed. As long as men are in the world of causes, they are all in a boat, and all asleep; waiting for what their soul shall see in sleep, of what awaits them of reward and punishment.

A fierce fire means the heat of anger; a spring of water is a beloved child.

To weep in a dream is a provision of happiness afterwards; slavery means immunity from disgrace. Playing at draughts or chess in sleep brings war and conquest and misery.

Water in a dream, if it be pure and sweet and clean and wholesome, is daily bread lawfully earned; but if it be muddy, know that it means an unhappy life;--though it be water, deem it fire itself. Earth in a dream brings food; to the farmer it indicates prosperity. A wind, if it be either hot or cold, is equally a store of grief and pain., but if it be temperate to the skin it is grief to an enemy and joy to a friend.

To give anything to the dead in a dream is loss of wealth and property. Laughter is anxiety and dangers; silence is affection for one's wealth. To drink water and have one's thirst increased is knowledge, for one is never satiated with it. And he who is naked in his dream falls into disgrace, like the drunken libertine. A drum in a dream,--the secret leaks out; a trumpet in a dream results in a quarrel. Bonds and fetters area repentance of Nasûh; to see a garden is food for the soul. Fruit in a dream is a stipend from the king, not at once, but at some future time; when the time comes for him to obtain it, the man who saw the dream will attain thereby to affluence.

When a man sees his own hand outstretched, he will be of singular generosity and munificence; but if his hands be withdrawn, he will surround himself with an army by his stinginess. The hands are brother and sister, the left the girl, the right the boy; the fingers represent sons; the teeth refer to father and mother; daughters are represented by the breast and nipple. Hidden wealth and riches are shown as the belly; in a dream, the liver and heart are a store of wealth. The leg and knee are weariness and trouble. The brain is hidden wealth; the side a woman, for veil the skin drawn round her body. The organ of generation is a son,--good or bad, ugly or fair, wretched or fortunate.

To wash the hands is despair in regard to the matter in hand: to dance is impudence and deceit. Bathing drawers and can and implements of bathing all point to servants; and he who in his dream plays upon the lute will certainly marry in haste. To wrestle with another is to conquer and to harass; and he who takes medicine in his dream escapes from pain and sorrow and torment.

Perfume in a dream is of two kinds, one meaning pleasure, the other nothing but affliction; the kind that is rubbed on brings pleasure, that which they scatter about, trouble. Since by smoke is meant an increase of trouble, such an one's comfort will be small compared with his distress. A sick man, and perfume, and a new coat, is bad, the bad that I represent to thee as good. To dance in a boat in a dream means danger from drowning, and brings wretchedness; but for one who is in prison, to dance is of good omen.

Whoever sees blood running from his body will find that happiness is denied him; permitted him, however, if he does not see a wound; but otherwise, if a wound be there, his affairs will cause him heavy trouble; he will be captive in sorrow's hands. And if a woman dreams of menstruating, she will give birth to a dead child. If a sick man seeing meat in a dream, eats of it, hope not for his recovery. To dream of drunkenness and madness from drinking wine, if it be Arabian wine, is bad; if Persian, deem it a livelihood, honour, and good-fortune. Milk in a dream is profit from one's possessions, an ample and lawful subsistence.

## ON DREAMS OF VESSELS AND GARMENTS.

An old garment is grief and sorrow; a new garment is great wealth; best of all is a garment that is closely woven, so my master told me. For women, a garment of many colours is a cause of joy and happiness and honour. A red garment brings gladness and the unrestricted enjoyment of a lasting good-fortune. The garment of fear is black; if yellow, it is pain and trouble and sighing; blue clothes are grief, a sorrow heavier than a mountain on the heart. Mantle and cloak are beauty; purse and moneybag are a source of riches.

A ladder will result in a journey, but one full of danger for the man. A millstone is a trusty man, the chosen one of a house. A snare in a dream is a block in the business in hand. A mirror is a woman; be well on thy guard. Captivity is plainly shown thee by a lock; so by a key thou obtainest thy release.

## ON DREAMS OF HANDICRAFTSMEN.

A cook means great riches, just as a butcher means that one's affairs are. ruined. A physician is pain and sickness, especially to one who is wretched and needy. The tailor is the man in virtue of whom troubles and affliction are all changed to good-fortune. A bootmaker and shoemaker and cobbler are among the heritages of one who will possess a secret. A draper, a goldsmith, and a druggist mean a successful undertaking and great wealth. A vintner, a musician, and a dancer bring, joy and gladness; a horse-doctor and horse-breaker and oculist point like a finger-post to ruin. To see a hunter in a dream brings trickery and deceit into one's path. A maker of swords indicates affliction; so too an arrow-maker, preparing arrows. A water-carrier, a potter, and a porter, all three are to be considered as indicating wealth.

## ON DREAMS OF BEASTS.

An ass is a servant, but a lazy one, who refuses to work. A horse, O thou of unparalleled wisdom! is a woman; both are suitable possessions for a man. A mule is bad for him whose wife is pregnant; a child will not be born to him. A journey comes to thee in a dream as a camel,--a terrible journey, grievous and painful. A cow points to a year of plenty; the owl grows arrogant before the king.

## ON DREAMS OF WILD ANIMALS.

A lion is a powerful and haughty adversary whose actions show no regard for humanity. An elephant is a king,--but a terrible one, whose rage is feared by all. Fortune and wealth come before thee as a sheep; a year of plenty demands the same sign. A goat signifies men mean and base by nature, clamorous, full of wickedness in their actions. A bustard is in every way advantageous;-this is no more than my master's words. The deer, O aged in wisdom! rather receives its interpretation from the women's apartments. The leopard, of evil deeds, represents an enemy perfidious in his dealings; the tiger also is considered to be an enemy,--so they relate in the book. The bear is a treacherous adversary, and a robber; no one will come by any good from seeing him. A hunting-leopard and hyena and wolf and fox are enemies, evil-disposed every one of them. And although the fox is a worker of wiles, yet it is still worse if thou see one dead. Every snake is a rancorous enemy; but again it is worse for thee if it makes towards thee. A scorpion and tarantula and other creeping things all and each denote calamities. Though in waking life a dog is a shepherd, in a dream it means war.

## ON DREAMS OF LIGHTS AND STARS.

To see the sun in a dream is said in every case to mean a king. The moon is as a counsellor; another has said, No, it is a woman. The globe of Mars or Saturn in a dream brings trial and grief and torment; Mercury represents a writer; Jupiter comes as a treasurer and minister of state; Venus is the origin of joy, of pleasure, of desire and of ease. And the other stars deem thou brothers; when thou interpretest them pronounce them such, for thus Ya`qûb, who established this method of interpretation, disclosed the secrets of this science to his son; the sun and moon were his father and mother, the stars represented his brothers.

Has anyone seen the sorrowing ones perplexed like we have? Now we will leave the dreams of those who wake; to awaken a sleeper is easy, but the heedless is like one dead. Make an end of divination and augury and interpretation: pass hence,--thou hast finished thy recital.

# ON THE INCOMPATIBILITY OF THE TWO ABODES.

The sun and earth produce the day and night; when thou hast passed beyond, neither the one nor the other will exist for thee.

O thou in whose imagination desire and desirer are two, know that the duality belongs to thy understanding, and belongs not to the Unity. Since in the Presence of One such as He all things are one, if thou wilt listen to my words, then seek not thou duality; know that in duality is pain and opposition, in Unity Rustam and a catamite are alike.

Till on the battlefield of purity and in the court of the soul, standing above thy life and treading on thy earthly body, thou cast away thy sword, thou wilt not become a shield; till thou lay aside the crown thou wilt not become a leader. So long as thy soul is a slave to the crown, thy acts will ever be wrong; when thou no longer heedest crown and zone, then art thou chief over the chiefs of the age. To abandon the world is to mount the horse of God's favour; its repudiation is the establishment of pure truth. The death of the soul is the destruction of life; the death of the life is salvation for the soul. By no means stand still on this path; become non-existent,--non-existent too as regards becoming non-existent; when thou hast abandoned both individuality and understanding, then for thee this world changes to that one.

Every desire that springs up in thee, strike that moment at its head, as thou dost with the lamp, the candle, and pen; for every head that comes in sight is on this Path meet to be cutoff. To be headless before heroes is due respect; for ever a chief seeks a cap of honour. To lose thy head brings thee a head again for its fruit; by reason of its headlessness the pomegranate is a casket full of pearls.

Though a crown is a protection to a bald head, with such a head it is wrong to wear a crown. Thou hast corruption under thy cap, --then canst thou not possibly pass the bridge of fire. Better for a man than earthly fortune is a well; a bald man becomes arrogant when he receives a crown; so is it well that while on this night-journey, when thou puttest thy hand to thy head, thou shouldest find no crown thereon; for while the baldheaded man desires a crown to cover his defect, the man of the Path seeks for the invisible. If the crown hurts thee, no less too inverted it destroys thy life; the head that is a slave to the crown is a prisoner, like Bîzhan, in a well. Then own neither head nor crown on the Path; if thou dost, thou wilt have thy heart aflame like wax; and if thou must needs have a crown, take one of fire, like the candle; for he who in his love is the light of the Path, like a candle has a crown of fire.

If thou demandest Yûsuf's place and power, invert thyself before God, like a well; guard like Sulaimân the perfectness of the Path: like Yûsuf look upon the well as beautiful; till thy bodily form becomes a dweller in the well, thy hidden figure will not be of God.

Arise, and leave this ignoble world to find the ineffable God abandon body and life and reason and religion; and in His path get for thyself a soul. Know, that whatso is of the true essence of learning and knowledge is all mere falsehood to him who is learned in attributes. Form, and attribute, and essence,--the first is like the womb; the next the membranes, the last the child; thy outward form covers in thy attributes, thy attributes again are a rampart around thy inmost essence; that, like a lamp, is bright in itself, while the other two are as a glass and a niche in the wall. Till on that road thou hast endured distress, thou hast two souls, though thy effigy is single. O thou, who art related to phenomenal existence but as soul is to body, whose soul is related to thy individuality but as a man to his name, exertion originates in the body, attraction in the soul; but the search begins in leaving both of these. Contingent existence is for ever an infant before the Eternal; but he who has been purified is free from these dregs. So long as the race of man endures, there are two mansions prepared for him; this, for pain and want, that one, for blessing and delight. While earth is the habitation of the sons of men, the tent of their daily supplies is erected over them; esteem then this earth a guest-house, but count man the master of a family; though till he has suffered pain on this dust-heap he will not reach the treasure of that mansion.

I ask thee, since thou art heir to the knowledge of philosophy and law, their principles and deductions, (religion ever flees from form, that she may constrain men from evil),--give me an answer truly, if thou art not dead, nor art asleep: Since thou hast been constituted with a soul, is not the soul a sufficient reward for thee in exchange for thyself.?

## THE PARABLE OF THE SCHOOLBOYS.

Thou knowest not the difference between the hidden world and this,--canst not distinguish between welfare and affliction. In truth, thou art not a man travelling on this Path; thou art a child of the Path, knowest not the Path; thou art but a boy,--go about thy play, go back to thy pride and independence. The airs and graces of thy mistress are enough for thee,--what, O son, hast thou to do with God? What concern hast thou with Paradise and eternal delight, who hast rejected the life to come for this present world? He knows thy baseness; how shall He invite thy thee-ness to Himself? He offers thee the virgins and palaces of Paradise, but thou art beguiled by this present world and its beauties. O unfruitful one! be not feebler than a boy to follow the path of God.

If a boy is unequal to learning his task, hear at once what it is that he wants; be kind to him and treat him tenderly; make him not to grieve in helpless expectation; at such a time give him sweetmeats in his lap to comfort him, and do not treat him harshly. But if he will not read, at once send for the strap; take hold of his ears and rub them hard; threaten him with the schoolmaster, say that he will have strict orders to punish him, that he will shut him up in a rat-house, and the head rat will strangle him.

In the path that leads to the life to come be not thou less apt than a boy to receive admonition; eternity is thy sweetmeat,--haste thou then, and at the price of two rak`ahs obtain Paradise. Otherwise the rat-house will for thee be Hell,-- will be thy tomb which meets thee on thy way to that other mansion. Go to the writing-school of the prophets for a time; choose not for thyself this folly, this affliction. Read but one tablet of the religion of the prophets; since thou knowest nothing thereof, go, read and learn, that haply thou mayest become their friend, mayest haply escape from this stupidity;--in this corrupt and baleful world deem not thou that there is aught worse than stupidity.

## ON STRIVING IN GOD'S PATH.

If thou wouldst possess the pearl, O man, leave the barren waste and wander by the sea; and if thou obtainest not from the sea its pellucid pearl, at least thou shalt find that thou hast not failed to reach the water. Strive in God's path, O soldier; if thou hast no ambition, thou shalt have no honour; saddle and get ready thy horse for the journey to the Court of the Blest. The man who disowns in shame the dust and water of his being rides on the air like fire; crown not thy head with the heavens, so mayest thou receive the diadem from Gabriel; thine shall be the angels' crown, while the crown of the firmament shall be cast down.

The true believer ever labours; for merely to hint at labour is a sick man's prayer. What knowest thou of contempt of life, having no will to show thyself a warrior? When thou hast laid low the head of pride then hast thou prostrated thyself before the door of the search; the heart's ka`ba has become God's dwelling-place. But the dog's ambition extends only to its bone.

## ON CHARITY AND GIFTS.

Whatsoever thou hast, relinquish it for the sake of God; for charity is the greater marvel when it comes from beggars. Bestow thy life and soul, for the endeavour of the poor is the best gift of mortal clay; the prince and chief of the family of the cloak was honoured by the Sûra "*Does there not come*,"--such regard he found with God from those three poor barley-cakes.

## OF THE STORY OF QAIS IBN `ÂṢIM.

When the command of *'Who is there that will lend'* (Qur. 2:246) came down from God to the Prophet, everyone brought before the Prince what he could lay hands on, not disobeying,--gems and gold, cattle and slaves and goods, whatever they possessed at the time. Qais b. `Âṣim was a poor man, for he sought no worldly gain. He went into his house, and spoke with his family, concealing nothing of what he had heard:--Such a verse has been revealed to-day; rise, and do not make me burn in waiting; bring whatever is to be had in the house, that I may present it before the Prince. His wife said, There is nothing in the house,--you are not a stranger here. Said he, Seek at least for something; whatever you find, bring it to me quickly.

She went and long searched the house, to see if by chance something would turn up; and found in the house a measure of dates, bad ones, and dried up, not fit for food, which she straightway brought to Qais, saying, We have nothing more than this. Qais put the dates in his sleeve, and brought them joyfully before the Prophet. When, not meaning a jest, but in all seriousness, he entered the mosque, one of the Hypocrites said to him, Bring it in; come, present quickly what thou hast brought; are they jewels, or gold, or silver, these valuables that thou art entrusting to the Prince? At this speech Qais suddenly became ashamed.

Look now what was the outcome. He went into a corner and sat down sorrowing, folding his hands together in shame. Gabriel the trusty came from the sidra-tree and said, "O lord of time and earth, do not keep the man waiting, and deem not contemptible what he has brought. He acquainted Muṣṭafâ with the matter, and, *'Those who defame the willing ones'* (Qur. 9:80) was thereupon revealed. The angel world came and looked on,--how they watched the man! An earthquake fell upon the angel world,--no place of rest, no place of peace. God Most High thus speaks, and in His kindness seeks out Qais's heart: O exalted, and O chosen as my Prophet, accept forthwith this much from Qais, for before me these poor dates show better than the others' gold and gems. I have accepted this small merchandise from him, because he has no date-palm. Of all the choicest things the endeavour of the poor is most approved.

Hence it was that Qais's act triumphed over the deed of that evil-spoken hypocrite. The hypocrite was straightway humiliated, and Qais's work thus completed; that thou mayest know that whoso comes forward, even in the state he is, does well. He who acts the hypocrite towards God is shamed by all his works. Sincerity is better than all else,--thou wilt at least have read so much.

An alms of a single diram from the hand of a darwîsh is more than a thousand dirams of the wealthy; forasmuch as the darwish's heart is sore, the alms he gives from his sore heart is greater than the other's. See the rich man, how his soul is dark and clouded, like his clay; the darwish's clay is for ever pure, his soul is imperishable essence of gold. Hear what God's bounty has said: but to whom shall I tell it, for no one bears me company?--to the king of kings and lord of 'But for thee' He said "Nor let thine eyes be turned from them." (Qur. 18:26)

## ON INTIMATE FRIENDSHIP AND ATTACHMENT.

There is no injury in the world for thee like thy prosperity; there is no such enduring imprisonment as thy existence: 'the light has appeared' it is that bestows favours, 'the lie has failed' is both life and body. Wishest thou the Invisible? take Self out of the path, what has imperfection to do with the mansion of Invisibility? Thou art full of fault, yet intendest the invisible world;--it is above all impossible in incredulity and doubt. The chains of thy selfhood will not fall from the two feet of thy nature under the compulsion of thy folly; when thy being appears to thee as a veil, thy understanding will have fallen under thy anger.

Abandon talk, and bid farewell to thy lower self; if thou canst not, then turn thy two eyes into rivers, day and night in thy separation from God grieve over thy understanding, no longer employ it to meditate evil; free it from this tether,--then has thy task become easy for thee. When thou findest thy sustenance in the Soul, thou wilt look out on the land from the window of the angel world.

How long wilt thou say, "What is the arriving? In the path of religion what is it to be chosen?" Lay bonds upon thyself, then wilt thou be chosen; plant thy foot upon thy head,--then wilt thou have arrived. As long as thou art a biter, thou art not chosen; whilst thou inclinest to this world, thou hast not arrived. How shall a true son of Adam be such a biter as thou, or how shall devil or wild beast rend as thou dost? Thou art ever heedless and arrogant, a beast of prey and a devil, far removed from man's estate; like a tiger ever malevolent; the people of the world in distress through thy evil disposition. Upon this high road of debasement thou wilt attain to Self,--thou wilt not attain to Him.

The Kufan has given forth but one verse about the _S̱ûfî_; what has Love to do with the decision of Quraishite or Kufan; or the _S̱ûfî_ and his love with 'Further, it is in the tradition,' with negation and affirmation, and '_It is lawful_' and '_It is not lawful_? The _S̱ûfîs_ have lifted up their hands, and for '_Yes_' have substituted '_No._' The earth-scatterers in the bridal-chamber of His affection, and those who sit by the road which leads to the cell of His sanctity, all are moon-bright signs on the curtain of jealousy, immersed in tears from foot to head; all are recipients of His clemency, all captive to the knowledge of Him. Lay down thy burden of Self, that so thou mayest become the beloved of every street. The pure eye sees the purity of religion: when the eye is pure, it sees purely. Those who are not steadfast in Him are covered with dust; those who wear His crown are kings indeed. Take off thy head this many-coloured cloak; hold to a garment of one colour, like `Isâ, (_Jesus_) that like him thou mayest walk upon the water, and make of sun and moon thy fellow-travellers. Take all of self away from thyself, and then with that same breath speak the story of Adam. Till thy Self becomes small as an atom to thee, thou canst not possibly reach that place; that desire will never harmonize with Self; rise, and without thy Self pursue thy path.

## HE WHO IS INDIFFERENT TO THE WORLD FINDS A KINGDOM THAT SHALL NOT WANE. (Qur. 20:118)

There was an old ascetic in Baṣrâ, none in that age so devout as he. He said, I rise every morning determined to fly from this vile Self. My Self says to me, Come, old man, what wilt thou eat this morning? Make some preparation, come, tell me what I am to eat. I tell him, Death; and leave the subject. Then my Self says to me, What shall I put on? I say, The winding-sheet. Then he questions me, and makes most absurd requests, such as, O thou of blind heart, where dost thou wish to go? I say to him, Silence! to the grave-side; so that perhaps while in rebellion against my Self may draw a breath in freedom from the fear of the night-watchman.

Honour to him who contemns Self, and does not permit it to stand before him.

## ON THE ASCETICISM OF THE ASCETIC.

An ascetic fled from amongst his people, and went to the top of a mountain, where he built a cell. One day by chance a sage, a learned man, wise and able, passed by and saw the ascetic, so holy and devout. Said he, Poor wretch! why hast thou made thy dwelling and habitation and home upon this height? The ascetic said, The people of this world have been clean destroyed in their pursuit of it: the hawk of the world is on the wing, calling aloud in every country; he speaks with eloquent tongue, seeking his prey throughout the world, ever calling on its people afflicted and parted from their lord, Woe to him who fears me not, who shows no anxiety to seek me! Let it not happen as in Fusṭâṭ--few birds and hawks in plenty!

## ON THE LOVE OF THE WORLD AND THE MANNER OF THE PEOPLE OF IT.

There is a great city within the borders of Rûm, where a large number of hawks have made their home. Fusṭâṭ is the name of that city of renown; it extends to the borders of Dimyâṭ. Within it no house-sparrows fly, for the hawks hunt them through the air and leave no birds inside that city, for they devour them within an hour. The times are now become like Fusṭâṭ; the wise are like the birds, despised and helpless.

I have hidden myself upon this height to be at peace from the evil of the world. The sage said, Who lives here with thee? How farest thou on this hill-top? Said the ascetic, My Self is in this house with me by day and night. The sage said, Then hast thou accomplished nothing; cease, O fool, to follow the path of asceticism. The ascetic said, They have fixed my Self within me, and sold me into his hands; I cannot separate myself from him--what means of escape could I contrive? Said that worthy philosopher to the ascetic, Thy Self instructs thee in evil deeds. The ascetic said, I have come to know my Self, and so I am able to get on with him; he is a sick man, and I am m it were his physician; day and night I look after him and am busy treating him, for he keeps saying he is indisposed. Sometimes I determine to bleed him, and open the vein before his eyes; as the blood spouts out, he subsides, and the bleeding calms him. Sometimes I give him a purge to clear out his distempers; and his love of the world, and hatred, and rancour, and envy, and treachery, and deceit are expelled from his body; on taking it he thrusts aside his natural inclinations and shuts the door of desire against himself. Sometimes I forbid him to indulge his appetites, that haply he may relinquish pleasure; I feed him on two beans, and make the room like a tomb upon him. Sometimes I put my Self to sleep, and then in haste make one or two obeisances; but even before he awakes from his sleep he clings to me like a sick man; and when I have got through one or two obeisances without him, then my Self wakes up.

On hearing these words the sage tore his garments one by one upon his body and said, How excellent art thou, O ascetic! May God bless thy life, thou pious man! Such words are granted but to thee; thy wealth is not less than the kingdom of Jam. That which thou possessest today is adornment, and what thou mayest have tomorrow, impurity.

He is not stained who leaves his sins, from whom in sorrow a sigh of 'Alas' arises:, a woman nimbly adorns her eyebrows and her ringlets for a feast.

In three prisons, deceit and hatred and envy, thou hast made thy understanding captive to thy body. The five senses, having their origin in the four elements,

III

are the five tale-bearers of these three prisons. The soul is a stranger here, and a fool, so long as it is in bondage to the four elements; how can the soul that is admitted to the treasury of the secret pay honour to spies and informers? But here wisdom empties the quiver, for persistence in one's purpose is useless at the Ka`ba. Haply a fool at the Ka`ba, will hear much philosophy about the direction of the qibla; but at the Ka`ba whoso should strive even till he died would but take fresh cuminseed to Kirmân. His tongue the tongueless speak; some mark of Him those seek who have no mark. Cast in the fire all else besides the Friend, then raise thy head from out the water of Love. On the journey from this life to the next the slave has no ally in what he does of right or infamy; surrender not thy heart and thy desire to the companionship of men; cut thyself off from them, lest they cut thy throat. At the last day thou shalt weary of men, but thou art far off now, and it will take thee long to come; then wilt thou discover the onion's value, when thou art denied admittance to the straight road. Those who are not friends, yet whom thou deemest such, thou wilt see that they all break their faith with thee. The rose-tree of the garden of those who cherish Self is become as a boil, a malignant pimple. Understand well, the state of men will be no whit different at the resurrection; whatsoever he chooses, that will be set before him, and what he takes from here he will see there. When the second command of God has uttered four *takbîrs* upon thy three pillars, the cloth-weavers of the eternal world will recite thine own words and poems to thee. The things the worthy shopkeeper sends to his house from the market, whatever they may be, his family bring before him at home in the evening; so whatever thou takest away from here is kept, and the very same is brought before thee at the resurrection. There is no change or substitution there; by no possibility can an evil become a good. Nothing will be given free to anyone there; what is due is given, and nothing besides. Rise and read, if thou knowest it not, the explanation of this in the Divine Word; 'thou shalt not find any change in the ordinance of God, thou shalt not find any alteration in His religion.' No alteration comes over His inexorable sentence, no change upon His all-embracing decree. Rise, and put away thy uncleanness, or thou wilt not receive thy pardon in that world; if now thou piercest thy Self with an arrow thou wilt throw into the fire thy sorrow and thy pain.

## OF ADDRESSES TO GOD, AND SELF-ABASEMENT, AND HUMILITY.

Prayer will not draw back the veil of Majesty till the servant comes forth front his defilement; as thy purity opens the door of prayer, so know that thy corruption locks it against thee. When wilt thou plant thy foot upon the heavens' roof, when drink wine from the angels' cup? How can God in His kindness take thee to Himself, or freely accept thy prayers, while like an ass within this rotting mansion thy belly is full of food and thy loins of water? How wilt thou ever see the Lord of the divine Law, thy lower parts sunk in the water and thy nose in heaven?

Thy beggar's food and cloak must both be pure, or thou wilt come to thy destruction in the dust; if food and raiment be not pure how is thy prayer better than a handful of dust? Keep pure for the glory of God's service thy habitation and thy raiment and thy soul; the dog sweeps his lair with his tail, but thou sweepest not with sighs thy place of prayer.

Though all thou hast be spotless, yet is all polluted before God. He who seeks Him makes use first of a bath, for God accepts not the prayers of the unclean; and how canst thou perform thy neglected ablution so long as thy heart holds enmity and hatred? Thy envy, anger, avarice, desire, and covetousness,--I marvel indeed if these will admit of thy coming to prayer! Till thou banishest envy from thy heart, thou wilt never be free from its evil workings. If thou hast not washed thyself free from blame, the mighty Lord will not receive thy prayer; but when thy heart draws thee out from thyself, then true prayer rises up from thy destitution. The whole of prayer lies in ablution and purification; recovery from a grievous sickness depends on the use of remedies.

Until thou sweep the path with the broom of *Not*, how canst thou enter the abode of *Except God*? So long as thou art under the dominion of the four, the five and the six, thou shalt not taste of wine save from the jar of lust. Burn and destroy all else but God; cleanse thyself from everything but the true faith. The soul's qibla is the threshold of the Most High; the heart's Uhud is the sanctuary of the One; at Uhud devote thy life like Hamza, that so thou mayest taste the sweetness of the call to prayer.

Come not in thy pride to prayer; take shame to thyself and stand in awe of God; him God receives in prayer who has no commanding dignity in his own eyes. Helpless, thou wilt be received with kindness; wanting for nothing, thy prayer will not be accepted. Wanting for nothing, if thou give thyself the trouble of prayer, thou shalt consume thy liver fried in the pan with onions. But if along with prayer goes helplessness, the hand of kindness shall raise the veil of the secret; then, speeding into the Court of God's kindness, he renders what is due, he obtains what he sought; and if it be not so, Iblis will hear thee when thou art at prayer, and drag thee forth again.

Thou camest abject, thy prayer is honoured; thou camest as a raw youth, thy prayer is as one of venerable age. Know, that the seventeen rak`ahs of prayer given forth from the soul's heart are a kingdom of eighteen thousand worlds; a kingdom of eighteen thousand worlds belongs to him who performs the seventeen rak`ahs; and say not that this reckoning is too small, for seventeen is not far from eighteen. Thy self-esteem utters no prayer, for it -sees no profit for thee in religion; while thy self-esteem guides the reins I doubt indeed if it will ever come where Gabriel is. Thy prayer will not admit thee to God if thou hast not purified thyself in indigence; thy purification ties in lowliness and selflessness, thy atonement in the slaughter of thy Self; and when thou hast slain thy Self upon the path, God's favour will quickly manifest itself. Come in thy poverty if thou wouldst find admission; and if thou do not so, then thou wilt quickly find thyself trebly divorced; for the prayer that is received into His presence has no concern with the pollution of worldly glory.

When death drags forth thy life, then from thy indigence there springs true prayer; when thy body has gone to the dust and spirit to the skies, then mayst thou see thy soul engaged, as angels are, in prayer.

# ON THE PARTICIPATION OF THE HEART IN PRAYER.

At the battle of Uhud `Alî the Prince, the impetuous Lion, received a grievous wound. The head of the arrow remained in his foot, and he knew that it was necessary to take it out, this being the only cure for him. As soon as the surgeon saw it, he said, "We must cut it open with a knife; to find the arrow-head, a key must be applied to the closed wound." But `Alî had no strength to bear the insertion of the forceps; "Let it alone," said he, "till the time of prayer." So when he was engaged in prayer his surgeon gently took out the arrow-head from his limb, bringing it clear away while `Alî was unconscious of any suffering or pain.

O When `Alî ceased from prayer (he whom God called Friend), he said, "My pain is less,--how is that? And why is there all this blood where I have been praying?" Husain, the glory of the world, splendid above all the children of Mustafâ, answered him, "When thou enteredst into prayer, thou wentest up to God, and the surgeon took out the arrow-head before thou hadst finished thy prayer." Said the Lion, "By the most great Creator, I knew nothing of the pain of it."

O thou, who art welt known for thy prayers, who art commended before men for thy piety, pray in this wise and, discern the interpretation of the story; or else rise, and cease vainly to wag thy beard.

When thou enterest into prayer in sincerity, thou wilt come forth from prayer with all thy desire obtained; but if without sincerity thou offer a hundred salutations, thou art still a bungler, thy work a failure. One salutation is the same as two hundred one prostration in sincerity is worth thy standing erect a hundred times, for the prayer that is mere matter of custom is dust that is scattered by the wind. The prayers that reach God's court are those that the soul prays; the mere mimic is ever a mendicant, praying unworthily, without intelligence, since he chooses the path of folly. For on this path prayer of the spirit is of more account than barren mimicry.

When thou callest on God, bring supplication meet for Him, that His good pleasure may receive thee. From time to time, divided from the real and bound up in the phenomenal, thou comest to pray the obligatory prayers; calling not on God, without self-abasement, without humility, thou carelessly performest a rak`ah or two. Thou deemest it prayer,--I marvel if thou art listened to at all! Thou comest before God in thy pride,--how shall God hear thee when thou callest? Let thy prayer be free from Self, and He will accept it as pure; if it be smirched with Self He will not receive it. The message that the tongue of anguish utters is an envoy from this world of men to Him; when it is thy helplessness that sends the messenger, thy cry is '*O Lord*', and His is '*Here am I*'.

As a proud lord marches to the arms of his servants and slaves so thou layest the load of obligation on Him;--"I am *Thy* friend," sayest thou, "honour be mine!" Thou deemest thyself a friend, not a slave; is this the manner of a man of wisdom? Better were it, O son, that thou offer not such service to Him; go, strive not with Him. Without right guidance man is less than a beast; whoso is without guidance labours in vain. Have done with this service, thou fool! Never again call thyself a slave! If thou wert mighty in the world thou wouldst say what Pharaoh did, every word! who in his surpassing fatuity, and his supreme insolence and folly, averse from service and submission, drew aside the veil from before his deeds, saying, "I am greater than the kings, I am above the princes of the world." All have this insolence and pride; Pharaoh's words are instinct in everyone; but daring not through fear to utter their secret, they hide it away even from themselves.

## ON FAILURE TO PRAY ARIGHT

Bû Shu'aib al-Ubayy was a leader in religion whom everyone used to praise; one who rose in the night and fasted continually, one who was distinguished in that age for his asceticism. He betook himself from the city to a cell on the mountain, and made his escape from pain and sorrow.

It chanced that a certain woman had an affection for him; she said, "O Shaikh, would it be fitting for thee to have a wife? If thou wilt, I place myself at thy disposal, and will willingly become thy wife; my soul will cheerfully be satisfied with little, and. I shall never think of my former ease." He answered, "Excellent; it is very fitting; I approve. If thou art satisfied, I am content."

She was a modest woman called Jauhara, and had a full share of beauty and grace; chaste, refined, of sweet disposition, an incarnation of good deeds; content with the decree of the revolving heavens, she left the city for the hermit's cell, and there seeing a piece of matting lying on the floor, she straightway took it up. The

devout Bû Shu'aib said to her, "O thou, now my cherished wife, why hast thou taken up the carpet? For the black earth is only the place for our shoes." She said, "I did it because it was best so; for I have heard you say that any act of devotion is best performed when no screen interposes; and the mat was an obstacle between my forehead and the actual earth.

Every night Bû Shu'aib's daily meal consisted of two round cakes for his querulous belly; with these two barley-cakes that pious man broke his fast and was always content. But he fell ill from the risings that so affected his nights; and so, being helpless, the good man, because of the weakness brought on by fasting, said the *jarz* and *sunnah* prayers that night sitting. His wife laid one cake before him, and gave him a drop of vinegar,--nothing more. Said the Shaikh, "O wife, my allowance is more than this! Why is it so little, wife! She said, "Because the worshipper who says his prayers sitting receives only half the full reward; and if thou sittest to say thy prayers, thou eatest the half of thy usual allowance. Ask no more from me, O Shaikh, than half thy dole; I have warned thee. For the portion that belongs to prayers said sitting is the half of the reward given for those said standing; why expect the reward of the whole when thou performest but half thy devotions? Perform the whole, and then ask for the whole reward; otherwise such worship is absolutely wrong."

O thou, in the path of sincerity thou art feebler than a woman, laggest far behind such of thy fellow-creatures as she. By such prayer as comes not from the heart thou canst not anywise obtain thy soul's release. No one regards as of any worth the service whose life principle comes not from the heart; for a bone is of itself no delicacy on one's plate without the marrow. Know that at the resurrection no prayer that is imperfect will be taken into account; the marrow of prayer consists in lowliness, and if there be not lowliness it will not be received. A man must come to prayer as one wounded, sorrowing, and in poverty; and if there be not lowliness and trust the devil derides him.

Whoso is wholly taken up with fasting and prayer, poverty ever locks the door of his soul; in this world of deceit and desire, in this hundred-thousand-years-enduring cage, the cap of thy degree is the compliment thou offerest it; but thy head is greater than the cap.

Whoso enters into prayer with fitting preparation, the reward of his prostration is the eave of the West.

Go then, perform thy prayers without breath of desire, for the dew of desire utterly corrupts them; the baseness of thy prayers and thy fasting is such that the slipper of thy foot is the only present in thy hand. Speak in pleasant tones on coming to the mountain; why offer it the braying of an ass? Thou hast raised up a hundred thousand ruffians in the path of prayer, who drown thy cries. It must needs be that the words of thy prayer come back in their entirety, like an echo, from the mountain of the world.

## ON LAUD AND PRAISE.

In every mouth the tongue that utters speech becomes fragrant as musk in praising Thee. In Thy decree and will, as Thou art far or near, lies for the heart and soul eternal happiness or ruinous disaster, an imperishable kingdom or everlasting beguilement; Thy servants wander to and fro by day and night, all seeking Thyself from Thee. Fortune, and empire, and the glory of both worlds he knows who understands things manifest and hidden, yet longs not for them; for all is nothing without Thee,--nothing. Destruction and creation are alike easy to Thee; all that Thou hast willed, takes place. The cunning man, though mightier he be, is yet the feebler in Thy praise; or in this court Zâl-i-zar, though full of fury, is powerless as an old woman; in face of Thy decree of '*Be, and it was*,' no one dares to question, 'What is this? How comes that?'

## ON POVERTY AND PERPLEXITY.

He hears the heart's low voice of supplication. He knows when the heart's secret rises up to Him; when supplication opens the door of the heart, its desire comes forward to meet it; the '*Here am I*' of the Friend goes out to welcome the heart's cry of '*O Lord*' as it ascends from the high road of acquiescence. One cry of '*O Lord*' from thee,--from Him two hundred times comes '*Here am I*' one '*Peace*' from thee,--a thousand times He answers '*And on thee*'; let men do good or ill, His mercy and His bounty still proceed.

Poverty is an ornament in His court,--thou bringest thy worldly stock-in-trade and its profits as a present; but thy long grief is what He will accept, His abundance will receive thy neediness. Bilâl whose body's skin was black as a sweetheart's locks, was a friend in His court; his outward garment became as a black mole of amorous allurement upon the face of the maidens of Paradise. O Thou who marshallest the company of darwîshes, O Thou who watchest the sorrow of the sore at heart, heal him who is now like unto a quince, I make him like the bowstring who is now bent as the bow. I am utterly helpless in the grasp of poverty; O Thou, who rulest the affairs of men, rule mine. I am solitary in the land of the angels, lonely in the glory of the world of might; the verse of my knowledge I has not even a beginning, but the excess of in yearning has no end.

## ON BEING GLAD IN GOD MOST HIGH, AND HUMBLING ONESELF BEFORE HIM

O Life of all the contented, who grantest the desires of the desirous: the acts in me that are right, Thou makest so,--Thou, kinder to me than I am to myself. No bounds are set to Thy mercy, no interruption appears in Thy bounty. Whatever Thou givest, give thy slave piety; accept of him and set him near Thyself. Gladden my heart with the thought of the holiness of religion; make fire of my human body of dust and wind. It is Thine to show mercy and to forgive, mine to stumble and to fall. I am not wise,--receive me, though drunk; I have slipped, take Thou my hand. I know full well that Thou hidest me. Thy screening of me has made me proud. I know not what has been from all eternity condemned to rejection; I know not who will be called at the last, I have no power to anger or to reconcile Thee, nor does my adulation advantage Thee. My straying heart now seeks return to Thee; my uncleanness is drenched by the pupil of my eye. Show my straying heart a path, open a door before the pupil of my eye, that it may not be proud before Thy works, that it may have no fear before Thy might. O Thou who shepherdest this flock with Thy mercy,--but what speech is all this? they are all Thee. . . . . Show Thou mercy on my soul and on my clay, that my soul's sorrow may be assuaged within me. Do Thou cherish me, for others are hard; do Thou receive me, for others themselves are rent asunder.

How can I be intimate with other than Thee? They are dead, Thou art my sufficient Friend. What is to me the bounty of Theeness and doubleness, so long as I believe that I am I, and Thou art Thou? What to me is all this smoke, in face of Thy fire? Since Thou art, let the existence of all else cease; the world's existence consists in the wind of Thy favour, O Thou, injury from whom is better than the world's gain.

I know not what sort of man he is, who in his folly can ever have sufficiency of Thee. Can a man remain alive without Thy succour, or exist apart from Thy favour? How can he grieve who possesses Thee; or how can he prosper who is without Thee? That of which Thou saidst, Eat not, I have eaten; and what Thou forbadest, that have I done; yet if I possess Thee, I am a coin of pure gold, and without Thee, I am a mill-wheel's groaning. I am in an agony for fear of death; be Thou my life, that I die not. Why sendest Thou Thy word and sword to me? Alas for me, who am I apart from Thee?

If Thou receive me, O Thou dependent on no cause, what matters the good or ill of a handful of dust? This is the dust's high honour, that its speech should be in praise of Thee; Thy glory has taken away the dust's dishonour, has exalted its head even to the Throne. Hadst Thou not given the word of permission, who, for that he is so far from Thee, could utter Thy name? Mankind would not have dared to praise Thee in their imperfect speech. What is to be found in our reason or our drunkenness? for we are not, nor have we an existence.

Though we be full of self, purify us from our sins; by some way of deliverance save me from destruction. In presence of Thy decree, though I be wisdom's self, yet who am I that I should count as either good or evil? My evil becomes good when Thou acceptest it; my good, evil when Thou refusest it.

O Thou art all, O Lord, both my good and ill; and, wonderful to say, no ill comes from Thee! Only an evil-doer commits evil; Thou canst only be described as altogether good; Thou willest good for Thy servants continually, but the servants themselves know naught of Thee. Within this veil of passion and desire our ignorance can only ask for pardon at the hands of Thy Omniscience. If we have behaved like dogs in our duty, Thou hast found no tigerishness in us,--then pass over our offence. As we stand, awaiting the fulfilment of Thy promised kindness at the bountiful door of the Court of Thy generosity, on Thy side all is abundance; the falling short is in our works.

## ON HIS KINDNESS AND BOUNTY.

O Lord, the Enduring, the Holy, whose kingdom is not of touch or sense; by Thee we conquer, without Thee we fail; in Thee we are content, apart from Thee unsatisfied. Though none amongst us is of any avail, is not Thy kindness a sufficient messenger of promise? Thou hast given us our religion, give us a sure belief in it; though we have the faith, give us yet more. Checkmated on the chessboard of our passions as we are, we thirst for the heavenly valley; none of us can tell the good from ill,--give us what Thou knowest to be good. O Thou, desire of the desirous, O Thou, the hope of those who hope, O Thou who seest what is manifest, who knowest what is hidden, Thou surely accomplishest my hope; all my hope is in Thy mercy,--life and daily bread, all is of Thy bounty. From the river of the true religion give to my thirsty heart a draught full of the light of the Truth.

Not by wisdom and not by skill can I obtain other intercessor with Thee than Thyself. All that Thy decree has written for me is well; it is not ill. I can dispense with ever thine,--all that is; but Thou art indispensable to me; receive me Thou In the rose-tree of the search the nightingale of love trills its song of "Thou art all!" The falcon of my glory flies up from the path of lowliness higher than the sidra-tree. He rules empires who presses on towards Thee; but whoso makes not for this door, wretched is he.

Who shall give me speech but Thou? Who shall save me from myself but Thou? Thou buyest not perfume and paint and deceit; save me from all this, O Thou who art all! Thou buyest weakness and helplessness and feebleness, but not indolence and stupidity and uncleanness. Pain becomes ease at Thy court, silence is perfect eloquence. Kill everything (i.e., All our desires, passions, follies and impurities) and, for it all, to be received by Thee will be sufficient blood-money. To turn the reins of hope away from Thee,--what is that but the sign and mark of a fall? Thy vengeance takes shape in the soul of whoso seeks aught but to be beloved of Thy presence; O Guardian of the mysteries, save our inward nature from the impress which marks the wicked!

## ON TURNING TO GOD.

O Creator of the world, who preservest the soul in beauty; O Thou who guidest the understanding to the path of true devotion; in the Paradise of the skies they are all raw youths; in Thy Paradise are those who drink of Hell. What are good and ill to me at Thy door? What is Heaven to me when Thou art there? Who can show forth in this deceptive mirror, the import of the words "All-knowing" and "All-powerful"?

When the heart's blood bores the liver, what is Hell, what a baker's live coal? Hell would become Heaven through fear of Him; how can clay become a brick without a mould? Those who love Thee weep in their laughter because of Thee; those who know Thee laugh in their weeping because of Thee. They rest in Paradise who are in Thy fire; but the most are contented apart from Thee with the maidens of the eyes. If Thou send me from Thy door to Hell, I will not go on foot but on my head; but whoso opposes Thy decree, his soul shall hold up a mirror to him, because of his recklessness.

His standing and his occupation Thou givest to everyone; a friend is a snake,-- a snake a friend if sent by Thee. Though threatened with "*None will think himself secure*," I cannot have enough of Thee; nor do I become bold because of "*Be not in despair.*" If Thou givest poison to my soul, I cannot mention anything bitterer than sugar. He only is secure from Thy craft who is mean and lowly; Thy peace and Thy craft appear alike, but at Thy craft the wise man trembles. We must not think ourselves secure against Thy craft, for neither obedienee nor sin is of avail; he only thinks himself secure, who knows not Thy craft in dealing with wickedness.

## HE WHO TRUSTS IN HIS SUBMISSION SUFFERS A MANIFEST HURT.

An old fox said to another, "O master of wisdom and counsel and knowledge, make haste, take two hundred dirams, and convey our letter to these dogs." He said, "The pay is better than a headache, but it is a heavy and perilous task; when my life has been spent in this venture, what use will your dirams be then?"

A feeling of security against Thy decree, O God, is, rightly understood, the essence of error; it made both `Azâzîl and Bal`âm infamous.

## ON DEVOTION TO GOD.

Say "Grind sleep under the foot of the horsemen of thy thought:" for this is of Thy Court. When Thou strikest off the head of him in whom Self no long dwells, he rejoices in Thee, like a candle. If I have Thee, what care I for intellect, and honour, and gold? Thou art both world and faith; what care I for aught else? Do Thou give me a heart, and then see Thou my valour; call me to be Thy fox, and see how like a tiger I shall be. If I fill my quiver with Thy arrows, I grip Mount Qâf by loins and armpits. Thou art his Friend who is not knowledgeless; Thou belongest to him who belongs not to Self. No one who regards Self can see God; he who looks at Self is not one of the faith; if thou art a man of the Path, and of the true religion, cease for a time to contemplate thyself.

O God, Omnipotent, Forgiving, drive not Thy servant, from Thy door; make me Thy captive; take away my indifference; make me athirst for Thee,--give me not water! Why should I seek my soul in this or that? my pain itself leads me to Thee, my goal. Like an ass without headstall before its greens, thou now beginnest to employ thy worthless life. Thou idly wanderest from city to city; seek thy ass on that road where thou hast lost it. If they have stolen thy ass from thee in 'Irâq, why art thou to be seen in Yazd and Rai?

Till thou becomest perfect, there is a bridge for thee; when thou hast become perfect, what matters sea or bridge to thee? Let thy burden on this road be thine own right-doing and knowledge, and trouble not thyself about any bridge. Make not for the boat, for it is not safe; he who goes by boat knows nothing of the sea; it would be a strange sight to see a duck, however young and inexperienced, seeking for a boat. Though a duckling be born but yesterday, it goes up to its breast in the water. Be thou as a duck,--religion the stream; fear not the fordless sea's abyss; the duckling swims in the midst of the sea of 'Umân, whence the ignorant boatman turns back. O Lord, for the honour of Adam, confound these fools of the world!

If thou maintain thy foot in the path of the Eternal, thou wilt hold the sea in thy hand; the surface of the outer encircling ocean is a bridge to the foot that speaks with the Eternal.

## OF HIS MERCY.

Malice and rancour are far removed from His attributes: for hate belongs to him who is under command. It is not permissible to speak of anger in respect of God, for God has no quality of anger; anger and hatred are both due to constraint by superior force, and both qualities are far distant from God. Anger and passion and reconciliation and hatred and malice are not among the attributes of the one sole God; from God the Creator all is mercy; He is the Veiler of His slaves; of His mercy He gives thee counsel; He draws thee to Himself by the kindness of the noose. If thou comest not, He calls thee towards Himself, He offers thee Paradise in His kindness, but because thou livest in this abode of sorrow thou of thy folly hast taken the road of flight. Thou art as a shell for the pearl of the belief in the Unity; thou art a successor of the newly-created Adam; if thou lose that pearl of thy belief, in being dispossessed of it thou wilt be parted from thy substance; but if thou guard that pearl, thou shalt raise thy head beyond the seven (*planets*) and the four (*elements*); thou shalt reach eternal happiness, and no created thing shall harm thee; thou shalt be exalted in the present time, and upon the plain of eternity thou shalt be as a hawk; thy alighting-place shall be the hand of kings, thy feet shall be freed from the depths of the, mire.

## OF HIM WHO FEEDS ME AND GIVES ME DRINK.

When they capture the hawk in the wilds, they secure it neck and feet; they quickly cover up both its eyes and proceed to teach it to hunt. The hawk becomes accustomed and habituated to the strangers, and shuts its eyes upon its old associates; it is content with little food and thinks no more of what it used to eat. The falconer then becomes its attendant, and allows it to look out of one corner of an eye, so that it may only see himself, and come to prefer him before all others. From him it takes all its food and drink, and sleeps not for a moment apart from him. Then he opens one of its eyes completely, and it looks contentedly, not angrily, upon him; it abandons its former habits and disposition, and cares not to associate with any other. And now it is fit for the assembly and the hand of kings, and with it they grace the chase. Had it not suffered hardship it would still have been intractable, and would have flown out at everyone it saw.

Others are heedless,--do thou be wise, and on this path keep thy tongue silent. The condition laid on such an one is that he should receive all food and drink from the Causer, not from the causes. Go, suffer hardship, if thou wouldst be cherished; and if not, be content with the road to Hell. None ever attained his object without enduring hardship; till thou burn them, what difference canst thou see between the willow and aloes wood?

## OF THE MULTITUDE; THEY ARE LIKE CATTLE--NAY. THEY ARE MORE ERRING.

On the colt that is full three years old the breaker puts the saddle and bridle; he gives him a training in manners, and takes his restiveness out of him; he makes him obedient to the rein,--what is called a hand horse. Then he is fit for kings to ride, and they deck him with gold and jewels.

If that colt had not experienced these necessary hardships, he would have been of less use than an ass, only fit to carry millstones; and would have been perpetually in pain from his loads, bearing now the Jew's baggage, now the Christian's, in pain and sorrow and tribulation.

The man who has never undergone hardship has not, so think tile wise, received a full measure of blessing; he is Hell's food, is in terror; even in Hell he is no more than a stone; his is the place of fear and dread; it is read in His incontrovertible book, " *Whose fuel is men.*" (Qur. 2:22)

Though thou canst neither purpose nor compass aught without Him, yet religion's task is not to be accomplished without thee, ally more than without Him; religion's task is not all easy business, God's religion is always a thing of heaviness. God's religion is a man's crown and diadem; does a crown befit a worthless man?, Guard thy religion, so mayest thou attain thy kingdom; otherwise, know that without religion thou art a man of naught. Tread the path of religion, for if thou do so, thou shalt not tremble like a branch in nakedness. Sweet is religion's path and God's decree! leave the black mire, lift thy feet out of it.

## ON THE DESIRE FOR GOD

Thereafter the desire for God, existing in his heart and soul and reason and discernment, becomes his horse; when this creation has become a prison to him, his soul seeks freedom; a fire is kindled within him, which burns up soul and reason and religion.

So long as he seeks for love with self in view, there waits for him the crucible of renunciation; whoso has newly undertaken the way of love, his renunciation is the key of the gate. Desire, when it is joined to its mistress, is gladness, but he who seeks mistress is far from God. The legion of thy pleasures will cast thee into the fire; the following out of thy desire for God will keep thee safe as a virgin of Paradise.

Then when the soul sets forth from the gate, the old heart becomes new thereat; his form escapes from the bonds of nature, the heart gives back its charge to the spirit. From earth to God's throne comes forth a mighty shout by reason of his soul's progress; the dust raised by the wind of his desire and pain turns woman into man if it but pass by her. All that would cause him trouble in his way quits the path before him; before him the mountains in fear become coloured wool for his socks; the fire in him destroys the glory of the sea for the sake of his upward ascent. When he is roused to leave himself they throw down the stars before him; when his eye sees the brightness of the Path, the sun seems dark to him by its side. There is no evil or good in that world, no earth or sun or stars; but whoso walks not in love's street, nor in his heart seeks love, for him is made a different heaven, him they seat upon a different earth.

Because of the labour of his search Gabriel unceasingly bathes his face in the water of life. Understanding is bewildered by his soul's shout; devils become firewood for the lightning of his horse's hoofs; to pursue the path his pained heart would burn mankind with fire of sighs. None of the contented can know the secret of his sigh, none pious with earthly piety can ever find his footprints. When his horse's hoof scatters the dust, Gabriel makes of it a life-giving fragrance; as he makes towards the world of annihilation the wind cries 'Halt a moment'; Muṣṭafâ standing by his path in benevolence calls out 'O Lord, keep him safe!' Because of his high dignity God suspends the scales of justice from his heart; the friend of God sprinkles water in his path . Gabriel's self cracks the whip.

## ON HIS DECREE AND ORDINANCE AND HIS CREATIVE POWER.

All that comes forth in the world is by decree, and what the prophet speaks is also by decree; infidelity and faith, good and evil, old and new,--all is referable to Him; whatso exists, is under the command of the Almighty; all things work in accordance with the decree. All are in subjection,--His Omnipotence the subduer; His creative Power appears high above all. All is subject to His Omnipotence, dependent on His mercy; all were preceded in time by His eternal Omniscience. The man of the people, or he of the philosophers, he who is under command, or who is of the learned,--all must return to His Presence; whoso possesses power, it is of His favour. His causes have displaced Reason from her position; His methods of deriving one thing from another have cut off the soul's feet. The soul's relation to the world of life is like a blind man and a pearl of `Ummân. One showed a pearl to a blind man; the greedy fool asked him, 'How much wilt thou give for this pearl?' He said, 'A round cake and two fishes; for no one can discern ruby or pearl, why be angry?--except by the pearl of the eye. So, since God has not given me this pearl, do thou take away that other pearl, and talk no more folly. If thou dost not wish to be laughed at by the ass, take thy pearl to one who is skilled in pearls; as soon as he puts the sole of his foot upon the oyster, his art knows well its value." Understanding is a tent before His gate, the soul a soldier in His army; the soul from fear of being rejected by Him sweeps not the dust of His Court except by permission; all in place and time are His property, from the '*Be*' of His decree to the wicket of '*It was.*' His decree has commanded the service of His Court to all intelligences in the words '*Obey God*' from the vegetative to the reasonable soul all like slaves are seeking Him. Well thou knowest that on the plain of eternity without beginning works the hand of the creative power of God, the Great and Glorious. God's decree has caused power in every sphere to become pregnant with act; so that when the way of the membranes is opened, there comes forth that wherewith they were pregnant. How shall Existence rebel against Him, to whom non-Existence is obedient? One word of command awakened the Universe; all things came together into the circle.

The soul that obeys the command, and commands; the intelligence that understands the Qur'ân and gives us our faith; wisdom, and life, and abstract form,--know that all proceed from the decree, and the decree from God. When the sun's light falls upon the water, the quiet water is stirred into activity; the sun's reflection from the water falls upon the wall and paints the ceiling with beauty; know that that too, that second reflection, of the water on the wall, is a reflection of the sun. He has caused all things to return to Himself; for none can escape from Him. All things are, yet all are far from All; thou hast read in the Qur'ân "*All things return.*" (Qur. 42:53) From Him are evil and good, power and might; '*the sentence is not changed*' is His decree (Qur. 50:28). His decree changes not: man can only stand in wonder before it. He is all-powerful to do whatso He shall desire; whatso He wills, He does, for His is the dominion. He who, invested with His authority, is in His secrets, and he whom He compels to be His slave,--all are subjected or exalted according to His decree. Mankind heed not the good or evil; as to whatso has been, and whatso shall be, that only can they do which He commands. All that the Master has written and set forth, the boy in school cannot but read; if from His records He has written out a certain alphabet, he cannot turn his head away from it. Whether thou existest or not is naught to the workings of God in the path of His might and power: all is God's work,--happy is he who knows it.

Reason became the pen, the soul the paper; matter received form, and body was transformed into individual shapes. To Love He said, 'Fear none but me'; to Reason, 'Know thyself.' Reason is ever Love's vassal; Love's point of honour lies in scorning life. To Love He said, 'Do thou rule as king'; to human nature He said, 'Live thou in thy household; in sorrow make the elements thy food, and afterwards take in thy hand the water of life.' So that when the reasonable soul has made of it her riches, and expends it in the path of the Holy Spirit, that Holy Spirit rejoices in the soul, and the soul becomes pure as the Primal Reason. This is the soul's progress from life's beginning to its end. In view of thy religion to fly from poetry is better,--to shatter thy verse as thou wouldst an idol; for religion and poetry, though at present they are on all equality, are utterly foreign to each other. The things that are permitted to us, are forbidden to one who is ignorant of both of these; he appreciates the difference between prohibition and permission who looks on ease in the light of a wound.

## TO REMEMBER THE WORDS OF THE ALL-KNOWING LORD

RENDERS EASY THE ACCOMPLISHMENT OF THE AIM. GOD MOST HIGH HAS SAID, SAY, IF MEN AND JINNS CONSPIRED TO BRING THE LIKE OF THIS QUR'ÂN, THEY COULD NOT BRING ITS LIKE, NOT THOUGH THEY HELPED EACH OTHER. (Qur. 17:90) AND SAID THE PROPHET (ON WHOM BE MERCY AND PEACE), THE QUR'ÂN IS RICHES; THERE IS NO POVERTY IF IT BE GIVEN, AND THERE IS NO RICHES BESIDE IT. AND HE SAID (PEACE BE UPON HIM), THE QUR'ÂN IS A MEDICINE FOR EVERY DISEASE EXCEPT DEATH.

By reason of its beauty and its pleasantness the discourse of the Qur'ân has no concern with clang of voice or travail of the letter; how shall phenomenal existence weigh its true nature, or written characters contain its discourse? Thought is bewildered before its outward shape, understanding stupefied before the secret of its sûras; full of meaning and beautiful are its words and sûras, ravishing and enchanting is its outward form. From it earth's produce and the sons of the angel-world have ever drawn their strength and nurture; in the loosing of perplexities its hidden meaning is souls' repose and hearts' ease. The Qur'ân is balm for the wounded heart, and medicine for the pain of the sore at heart. Do thou, if thou art not a parrot nor a donkey nor an ass, surely hold the word of God to be the root of the faith, and the cornerstone of piety, a, mine of rubies, a treasure of spiritual meaning. It is the canon of the wisdom of the wise, the standard of the practice of the learned; to praise it is joy to the soul, to look on it is solace to the mind. Its verses are healing to the soul of the pious, its banner is pain and grief to the evil-doer; it has thrown the Universal Reason into affliction, has made the Universal Soul sit down in widowhood. Reason and Soul but hold men back from its true essence; the eloquent are impotent to rival its manner.

# ON THE GLORY OF THE QUR'ÂN.

Glorious it is, though concealing its glory: and a guide, though under the veil of coquetry. Its discourse is bright and strong; its argument clear and apt; its words are a casket for the pearl of life, its precepts a tower over the water-wheel of the faith; to the Knowers it is love's garden, to the soul the highest heaven.

O thou to whom, by reason of thy heedlessness and sin, in reading the Qur'ân there comes upon thy tongue no sweetness from its words, into thy heart no yearning from their comprehension,--by its exceeding majesty and authority the Qur'ân, with argument and proof, is in its inner meaning the light of the high road of Islâm, in its outward significance the guardian of the tenets of the multitude; life's sweetness to the wise, to the heedless but a recitation on the tongue,--phrases upon their tongue whose sweetness they cannot taste, while careless of their spirit and design.

There is an eye which sees the spirit of the Qur'ân, and an eye which sees the letter;--for this the bodily eye, for that the eye of the soul; the body, through the ear, carries away the melody of its words; the soul, by its perceptive power, feeds on the delights of its spirit. For strangers the curtains of majesty are drawn together in darkness before its loveliness; the curtain and the chamberlain know not aught of the king;--he knows who is Possessed of sight, but how can the curtain know aught of him?

The revolutions of the azure vault have brought no weakening of its power, no dimming of its lustre; its syntax and form, pronunciation and nunation, prevail from earth to Pleiades.

Now hast thou in thy daily provision tasted the nut's first husk the first skin is rough and harsh, the second is like the moon's slough, the third is silk, pale and fine, and fourth is the succulent cool kernel; the fifth degree is thy abode, where the prophets' law becomes thy threshold. Seeing then thou mayest delight thy soul with the fifth, why halt at the first? Thou hast seen of the Qur'ân but its veil,--hast seen its letters, which do but hide it; it does not reveal its countenance to the unworthy,--him only the letters confront. If it had seen thee to be worthy, it would have rent this subtle veil and shown its face to thee, and there thy soul might have found rest; for it heals the wounded heart, and medicines the disappointed soul; the body tastes the flavour of the dregs that it may live; the soul knows the taste of the oil.

What can sense see, but that tile outward form is good? What there is within, wisdom knows. Thou recitest the form of its sûras, and its true nature thou knowest not; but know, that to him who truly reads the Qur'ân, the feast it gives comes not short of the guesthouse of Paradise. It has made the letter its veil, because it is to be concealed from alien eyes; material existence knows naught of its inmost soul,--know, its body is one thing, its soul a thing apart; from its outward form thou seest but so much as do the common men from the appearance of a king.

Why deemest thou that the words are the Qur'ân? What crude discourse is thine concerning it? Though the letter is its bedfellow, it knows it not, no more than the figures on the bath; nor do the sleepers and the cut-purses I see, like those who watch, the spirit of the Qur'ân.

## OF THE RECITAL OF THE SECRET OF THE QUR'ÂN.

Tongue cannot tell the secret of the Qur'ân, for His intimates keep it concealed; the Qur'ân indeed knows its own secret,--hear it from itself, for itself knows it. Except by the soul's eye none knows the mea, surer of words from the true reader of the Qur'ân;--I will not take upon myself to say that thou truly knowest the Qur'ân though thou be `Uthmân.

The world is like the summer's heat, its people like drunkards therein, all wandering in the desert of indifference; death the shepherd, men his flock; and in this waste of desire and wretchedness the hot sand shows as running water. The Qur'ân is as the cool water of Euphrates, whilst thou art like a thirsty sinner on the plain of the Judgment. The letter and Qur'ân hold thou as cup and water; drink the water, gaze not on the vessel. Because it is summer, thy home seems to thee a mine of enmity; because the water is cold, the vessel of turquoise, thou usest not to fast. To the pure heart suffering will tell in a cry of anguish the secret of the pure Qur'ân; how can Reason discover its interpretation? But a delight in it finds out its inmost secret. Though the written characters are not of the word, the scent of Yûsuf is in his garment; the fair Yûsuf was cast away in Egypt, but the scent reached Ya'qûb in Canaan. The letter of the Qur'ân is to its sense as thy clothes to thy life; the letter may be uttered by the tongue, its soul can be read but by the soul. The letter is as the shell, the true Qur'ân the pearl; the heart of the free-born desires not the shell. Though its words are fair and finely traced, though the mountain becomes as carded wool before them, make music, of them in thy heart like Moses, not outwardly like the treble of the pipes. When the soul recites the Qur'ân it enjoys a luscious morsel; whoso hears it, mends his ragged robe. The words, the voice, the letters of the verses, are as three stalks in bowls of vegetables. Though the husk is not fair nor sweet, still it guards the kernel; but through thy impurity the mystery becomes a song, the word of God a tune through thy folly.

Whilst thou art in this tomb appointed for us, this residence contrived for us, in this world full of objects of pursuit, this abode of deceit, look with thy earthly sight upon the willow, and with thy soul upon the ṭûbâ-tree; read with thy tongue the letter, and the sense with thy soul.

Sacrifice, to honour the Qur'ân, thy reason before its discourse; reason is no guide to its mysteries; reason is impotent here. Thou art now shameless, deceitful; thou art not worthy to have the curtain of the mystery drawn aside; thou knowest naught of its secret, hast not yet arrived at `Arafât. So long as thou desirest pleasure and cherishest desire, play as a child,--thou art not man enough for this.

But when wisdom has conquered the world of desire, pure goodness succeeds to evil; the devil of passion flies to Hell, and Sulaimân regains his ring; the Qur'ân's secret routs the demon;--what wonder if he flies in terror from the Qur'ân?

Wait, for when the day of true religion dawns, the night of thought and fancy and sense flies away. When the veiled ones of the unseen world see that thou art stainless, they will lead thee into the invisible abode and reveal to thee their faces; and disclosing to thee the secret of the Qur'ân, they will withdraw the veil of letters. The earthy will have a reward of earth, the pure shall see purity. An understanding of the Qur'ân dwells not in the brain where pride starts up; the ass is dumb as a mere stone, and lends not his ear to the secret of God's word,--turns away from hearing the Qur'ân and pays no heed to the sûra's secret; but if the mind be disciplined of God it shall discover in the sûra the secret of the Qur'ân.

# IN THE RECITAL OF THE MIRACLE WROUGHT BY THE QUR'ÂN.

O thou, who hast got into thy palm but the ocean's foam, and of thy possessions hast made the semblance of an array; thou hast not laid hold of the pearl's true substance, for that thou art occupied only concerning the shell; withhold thy hand from these lack-lustre shells, and bring up the bright pearl from the ocean depths. The pearl without its shell is cherished in the heart, the shell without its pearl is clay to be thrown aside; the pearl's value comes not from the shell,--the arrow's value comes from its hitting the mark.

He who knows of his own sight the pebbles of the sea-bottom will not mistake sheep's dung for pearls of the sea; while he who stands aside on this stream's shore can lay no claim to its shining pearls.

The, lines of the Qur'ân are like unto faith's shore, for it gives ewe to heart and soul; its bounty and its might are as the encircling sea around the soul's world; its depths are full of pearls and jewels, its shores abound in aloes-wood and ambergris; knowledge of first and last is scattered from it for benefit of soul and body both.

Be pure, that the hidden meanings may appear to thee from out the cage of the letters, for till a man come forth from his impurity how can the Qur'ân come forth from its letters? As long as thou art veiled inside thy Self, what difference, to thee or to thy understanding, is between evil and good? In the letter of the Qur'ân is no healing for thy soul,--the goat grows not fat on the goatherd's call; nor soon nor late the water of his dream satisfies the thirsty one in his helplessness. Thou, who art in thraldom to pen and ink, canst not distinguish between face and veil; in the world of the Word at least, the word's outward characters are not esteemed to be its life.

When thou settest foot in that country. He will teach thee the alphabet of sincerity, and when thou shalt recite the alphabet of the faith thou shalt know sun and Pleiades for thy father and ancestors; such is the way of the loyal followers, and such too is the alphabet of the lovers.

Dark is the veil on the face of day; the verse of its conceits is very subtle. If thou wouldst have a treasure for thy soul and heart, recite with heart and soul a verse from it; that in it thou mayest find the jewel of the truth, the essential basis of thy faith; that thou mayest find the casket of the incomparable pearl, and know the pure gold from the silver; that glorious as the sun and moon there may appear to thee from behind the dark screen its own beautiful face, like a bride who comes forth lovely and joyous from out her gauzy veil.

# OF THE GUIDANCE OF THE QUR'ÂN.

It is the guide, and the lovers the travellers; it is a rope, and the heedless sit in the pit. Thy soul has its home at the pit's bottom; the Qur'ân's light is a rope let down to it; rise and seize the rope, so thou mayest haply find salvation; else thou art lost in the pit's depth,--flood and storm will destroy thee. Like Yûsuf thou art brought by Satan into the pit; be thy wisdom the glad tidings, thy rope the Qur'ân; if thou desirest to be as Yûsuf, and to enjoy high place, take hold of it and come forth from the well.

The wise use the rope to obtain the water of life, but thou makest ready thy rope to dance on it for daily bread. No one learns two letters of the Qur'ân in a thousand centuries with such an eye as thine; the understanding's arm turns about as does a wheel; body and soul are captives of thy passions. If thou desirest throne and crown and honour, why sittest thou for ever at the well's bottom? Thy Yûsuf is helpless in the well, thy heart reciting the sûra '*safah*'; (Qur. 2:12) make of sorrow a rope, of thy sighs a bucket, and draw up thy Yûsuf from the well.

## ON THE GREATNESS OF THE QUR'ÂN,--VERILY IT CONSISTS NOT IN ITS DIVISION INTO 'TENS' AND 'FIVES.'

To attract a handful of boys thou hast made its honour to consist in the 'tens,' and 'fives'; thou hast abrogated the authority of every verse which abrogates another, art still unlearned in its doctrines the intricate passages seem to thee plain, while in its plain teachings thou hast no faith; thou hast abandoned the light of the Qur'ân, and for the sake of the multitude hast made its outward form the tool of thy hypocrisy for a measure of barley and two plates of chaff. Now thou intonest its cadences, now recitest its stories; sometimes thou makest of it a weapon for strife; sometimes in thy irreverence throwest it into disorder, sometimes esteemest it a prodigy; now thou interpretest it according to thine own conjecture, and again determinest to the contrary of that; now in thy fancy thou takest the conclusion of its passages for the beginning, now absurdly turnest its meaning inside out; again thou expoundest it by thine own opinion, and explainest it according to thine own knowledge; amongst the thirty caskets of the Qur'ân thou wanderest not except with railing.

Sometimes thou sayest to a foolish friend, perhaps a lazy clothweaver, "If I write thee a charm, keep it clean, O youth, and soil it not; but there must be a sacrifice in the morning,--the blood of a black bird is required." All this deceit for a diram or two, a supper or a breakfast for thy belly!

Thou hast wasted thy life in folly; what can I say? begone, and shame to thee! Thou creepest into some mosque or other in thy appetite, thy throat full of wind, like a pipe or a bell; shame on thy religion and thy faith for this appetite! May either wisdom be thy portion, or death! Shame on thee for such a nature, such accomplishments and science,--they bring thee no esteem!

## ON THE ALLEGATIONS BROUGHT FORWARD BY THE WORD OF GOD.

Wait till the Qur'ân shall make complaint of thee before God on the judgment day, and shall say, How much falsehood has this deceitful one, whom Thou trustedst, I drawn forth from Thy truth!--shall say, O God, thou knowest both the manifest and the hidden; night and day he recited me loudly, and rendered not justice to a single word of me. Neither in grammar, nor meaning, nor pure pronunciation did I ever receive in the miḥrâb my due from him with honesty. He has a good voice when he intones, and his robe of mourning is a pretty blue; but however he boasted his claims in respect of me, he knew not the depth of my meaning, for beyond talk and clamour this crowd are unable to utter a word. He never pushed forwards his horse towards my private grounds,--could not distinguish my face from my veil; when he entered my street he showed in his discussions no worth but only worthlessness. He surrendered not his mind and soul to my words, but forced me in the direction of his own decision and desire; now he wounded me with the sword of his lusts, and again he fettered me in the snare of his passions; now he brought me to his drinking parties, and again sang me as a song; sometimes he would recite me by way of profanity, making a noise like an ass in his shamelessness; now he would break through the frigidity of my words with his amorousness, as a gimlet through wood; now like a professional story-teller with his cadences he would scatter my words abroad to the stroke of his plectrum. O deviser of schemes! I ask for a just decision on the day of judgment against such an affliction!

For the sake of blandishment in this transitory abode,--sometimes in the crowded street and sometimes at time of prayer, sometimes by thy words and sometimes by thy voice,--thou shinest but to attract admiration. The words that have been polluted by thee, though they be wise, yet are they folly; for though the breeze is pleasant and delightful, yet if it pass over ordure it is not so. Has not God by His command plainly denied His Qur'ân to the impure?

# ON THE SWEETNESS. OF THE QUR'ÂN.

How shalt thou taste the flavour and delight of the Qur'ân, since thou chantest it without comprehension? Come forth through the door of the body into the landscape of the soul; come and view the garden of the Qur'ân, that all things may appear before thy soul,--what has been, what is, and what shall be, the world's dry and moist, within and without, whatsoever has been created by '*Be, and it was*,' the decrees ordained by Him,--all will be made plain to thee through it. God's attributes shall obey thee, and shall truly recount their narrations before thee.

When the hearer hears God's word, the utterance of it causes him to tremble.' Till thou see with the eye of purity, how canst thou recite the sûra *Ikhlâs*? (Qur, 112:1)--a sûra like a cypress of Ghâtfar, its rhythm like the violets of *Tabaristân*. The Qur'ân's loftiness and sublimity, if thou ask thy preceptor, are as the throne and seat of God; its letters are the wings of the Spirit, the curtain of the Light; its diacritical points black moles on the checks of the virgins of Paradise. Regard thou in this wise its outward form, that so thou mayest understand the secret of its sûras; that it may place an *alif* in thy mind, and put *bâ* and *tâ* underneath thy feet; and, for the sake of life and wisdom, may dispose of thy fair Yûsuf for eighteen worthless pieces, (Qur. 12:20)--for in the street of the love of Unity and true wisdom beauty is valued no higher than this.

The crucible of desire shall try him, and afterwards he shall be made like gold of the mine; yet again is the crucible prepared, that in it all fraud and deceit may be melted out; then when the pure metal becomes soft, it is polished and made an ornament for its possessor's crown. The diadem and crown of every lord of rectitude and faith are such as this.

## ON THE HEARING OF THE QUR'ÂN.

When the pious reader has set the book with reverence upon his lap, and has recited '*Let no one touch it*' (Qur. 56:78) over both his hands, for a single copper he gives forth a lusty cry, like a turtledove for a grain of corn. Hear God's word from God Himself, for the labour of the reader is only a veil. The Knower hears the word from the Truth; the force of his desire denies him sleep. The feelings may be captive to the professional reciter, but Love has its songster in the heart itself. Set a mole in thy inmost heart, and not upon thy cheek; for it is thy thoughts are the true index of thy state. The Qur'ân tells its secret to the discerning thought; turn and twist and pause are only matters of the voice, and whatso are matters of voice and written character and sound, reside outside the gate.

If there were any meaning in its song, a nightingale would not be sold for two coppers; seek for the essence of the matter in the meaning, not in the written words,--thou wilt find no scent in a picture of ambergris. The time of waiting in this transitory world deem but colour to the eye, and sound to the ear; but the session of the Soul is a place where hearing is not, and song is silence there. How shall Love deem worthy notice a sweet that can be tasted? Make not thy soul glad with song, for song brings no memories but of heaviness.

The friend who becomes thy friend at the bridge, take him not away from the water with thee; either drown him in thy hatred, or put him under ground, and then rest happy; but in Love, to bear the burden of its commands, whether good or whether evil, is wisdom. Give to the flames the gifts of the material world,--in thy smiling heart place instead of smiles a cry of lamentation; and when one of smiling heart gives forth a plaint, seize him by the foot and drag him off to Hell.

Knowest thou not, thou monster, that all those devils of thy lower nature, by using a hundred tricks and frauds and deceits, will break forth within thee, till thy reason and sense desert thee? O thou, who in this desert of injustice readest 'prosperity' for 'a whirlpool shame on thee! The path of religion consists not in works and words, not in syntax and accidence and metaphor; these kinds of things are far from God's word,--the contents of the Qur'ân are like scattered pearls. O Musalmâns, it may be the Qur'ân will one day depart again skywards; for though now its name is with us, its laws and commands are obeyed among us no longer.

The wise man listens to the Qur'ân with his soul, and abandons the letter and the outward elegance; his soul takes its delight in it, and sets to work afresh on all its duties. Know that to the eager disciple music and beating time are like poverty to a lover; the state of ecstasy that comes of skill and fraud is like the drowning cry of Pharaoh, his cry was useless to him as he drowned,--the fire of his reconciliation gave forth no smoke.

On the path, the condition of pursuing which is the devotion of one's life. foolish shouting is asinine and shameless whoso gives forth three shouts in the assembly, know that he does it in his anxiety for two coppers; but the sigh of the disciple who has gained Love is like a serpent sleeping upon a treasure; if the serpent raises himself upon the treasure, the pearl in his mouth darts forth fire. What is the darwish's laughter?--folly; and what the crackling of a lamp?--water. When water is mixed with the oil, the light, depending on the purity of the oil, is affected; when the oil begins to burn, the foreign moisture announces itself. Thy sighing is mere self-adornment, thy proper path is to observe God's law;--thy path is a polished mirror, but thy sighs veil it over.

## THE COMPARISON OF THE CREATION OF ADAM AND OF JESUS SON OF MARY (ON BOTH OF WHOM BE PEACE!).

Adam's father in this world was the same breath which begot the son of Mary; that which became his body was of the nature of humanity, and that which became his soul was of the fragrance of that breath. Whoso has in him that breath, is an Adam; and whoso has it not, is an effigy belonging to this world only. When Adam received that breath from the power of God his soul became conscious, and hastening towards the Universal Soul he asked, "What canst thou tell me of this breath?" Soul replied, "My cup and robe are empty; my robe and cup hold naught of it,--this precious gift has been given freely."

Wheresoever thou wilt incline, let it be in accordance with this breath; incline not towards thyself in opposition to it; and soar above the snares of earth, gaining the abode of Godhead, viewing the confines of the spirit-land, like Jesus, with the eye of thy divinity.

Claim no distinction for thyself in thy village, for thou art only distinguished in that to be naught is better than such distinction. Like a dot on the die used as a tool of the game, thou thinkest thyself to be something, but that something is naught; thou art indeed a unit, but like the dots on the dice hast a name merely for purposes of counting.

Fortunate is he who has effaced himself from the world; none seeks him, nor seeks he anyone. Whoso is caught in the bonds of this world, is a gainer if he escape from its forces; for this world is the source of pain and sorrow, and the wise man calls it 'the house of lodging.' Since in the light of reason and clear sight two flights at the proper time are as good as three victories, so thou, O full of excellencies, art a fool, if at this river thou stayest on the bridge or in the cave.

Let the guide of thy bodily and of thy spiritual life be for this world wisdom, for the other thy faith; fortunate is he whose guide is wisdom, for both worlds are his submissive servants. When the fruition of desire is attained, the go-between's talk becomes a heaviness; though she sets the business going, yet when the closet is reached she is only a bore to thee.

## TO COMMEMORATE THE PROPHETS IS BETTER THAN SPEAKING OF FOOLS.

The prophets were the upright ones of the faith, who showed to the people the path of rectitude; the self-opinionated were bewildered when they disappeared in the sunset of annihilation. The darkness of the night of polytheism drew close its curtains: infidelity placed kisses on the lips of idolatry; one bore a cross in his hand as it were a rose-branch, another like a waterlily worshipped the sun; one worshipped idols continually, and another had no aims whatever; this one in his senseless folly deeming evil from the devil, good from God; some strewers of dust, eaters of fire,--others beaters of the water, calmers of the wind; here one scouring all sense out of his brain, as it were done by wine,-- there another dashing the turban from his head, as if it were carried off by the gale; this one calling an image his god, and that one like the priest of an idol-temple wrecking all religion; one practising magic, another astrology,--one living in hope, another in fear; all were leading unlovely lives, all were blind of understanding.

The masses were suppliants to an impostor in the faith,--the magnates occupying the high places of religion; the religion of the Truth concealed its face, and everyone published a false faith; false doctrine and polytheism began to fly abroad, and every kind of heresy reared its head. Here one in bondage to the teachings of folly, there another satisfied with an empty deception; their ears listening to the devil's promptings of desire, their ravings displaying the devil's guidance. Folly and slander and idle chatter appeared wisdom alike to the crowd and to the wise; the great were the slaves of their lusts and pleasures, the populace of their jests and follies; the knowledge of God's religion was blotted out, all alike triflers, babbling folly; under pretence of knowledge each sought his own glory, and under cover of such knowledge each hid his reason. From fear of imposture and magic the virtues hid themselves, like the *alif* in *bism*, when the great withdrew to their houses, the people returned to their impieties. One followed the path of Moses, Jesus the leader of another; the faith of Zoroaster proclaimed itself, the veil of mercy was torn to pieces. The land of Tûrân and kingdom of Irân were each laid waste by the other's violence; the Ethiopians advanced towards Yathrib, the elephant and Abraha were routed by the birds. The house of the Ka`ba, seized by the stranger, became an idol-temple; the world was full of stupidity and fraud, the man of wisdom found the path of religion difficult. In this world of the lost ones dog and ass raised their voices every morning; it was a world full of the vile and worthless, `Utba and Shaiba and the cursed Bû Jahl; a world full of devil-like beasts of prey,--a hundred thousand paths with pits in the way, and all men blind; ghouls on either hand, in front a monster,--the guide blind, his companion lame; disabled by their ignorance, in the heaviness of sleep, the scorpion of their folly wards off from them the knowledge of their danger. Since somewhat has been said of the Unity, I will now speak of the glory of the prophets; especially the praise of the last of the apostles, the best and choicest of God's messengers.